Letters I wish I'd maile

to the man who di

to marry a wai

Letters I wish I'd mailed
to the man who divorced me
to marry a waitress

by

Andrea L. Emmons

VANTAGE PRESS

New York   Washington   Atlanta   Hollywood

This book is dedicated to Aniello,
my special Italian friend,
who gave me back my smile.

Acknowledgments

To protect the right of privacy valued by family members, friends, and professional people, changes were made in names, dates, and places as this story was written. For the same reason I have, as the author, used a pen name—one to which I feel a close and sentimental link.

I would like to thank the people who were there when I needed them. Words of gratitude sound stilted; still I want to thank the people who smiled and understood when I faced a most difficult time. We all need to remember that something so tiny as a smile, a touch, or a kiss given at the right moment may make all the difference in the world.

A. E.

Prologue

Being in my prime at the age of thirty-nine, I experienced a multitude of reactions when my husband, Andrew, told me softly and concisely that he no longer loved me. Andrew moved out of our three-car, eight-room house with two and one half baths, vacation for a month in Florida, see-a-dress-and-buy-it-without-looking-at-the-price-tag, two-income (almost twenty thousand dollars a year), upper-middle-class world. I found myself alone with a daughter, Leslie, just past sixteen; a son, Scott, slightly over eighteen; two dachshunds named Snoopy and Linus; six English classes with thirty students each; a million worries, fears, anxieties, and frustrations; a broken heart; and a venomous typewriter.

Half of my life had been spent married to one man. We had brought two children into the world, worked and scrimped to finish his bachelor's degree, his master's degree, my bachelor's degree, my master's degree, agonized through my learning to drive, and somehow in the process laughed and loved a great deal. He was a highly respected elementary principal, and I was a crazy, high-spirited, demanding English teacher. Leslie was a beautiful, compassionate high-school junior with many friends. Scott was a super intellectual, fighting windmills and alternating between knowing everyone and being a loner. It was his senior year. People described us as the ideal family group. We had gone through the early years of living on pancakes, potato soup, and peanut butter sandwiches. We struggled past the time of whipping up a dress out of an old drape to wear to the teacher's dinner. In every sense, the Helmans had arrived at the peak of the educational world for Middletown, Indiana. We were doing the things we loved. By all standards we were the family that had everything. When we divorced, the whole community was shocked because they could not believe it was happening to Adrianne and Andrew Helman. As a family we were too nice. Only one person was more shocked than the community, and that was myself. My adult life had started with three words when Andrew had said: "I love you." It seemed to end with five words when he said: "I don't love you anymore!"

It is now three years and one hundred and eighty-four letters later. I doubt if I will ever be able to say that I completely understand or that I completely accept what has happened. I can only say that at this point in my life I no longer have to write letters because I can cope without the bittersweet venom of the typewriter ribbon.

These letters are written for the thousands of women who suddenly or not so suddenly find themselves divorced. The reasons may be different, but the pain is seldom any less. It is my way of saying: "Hang on to your smile, baby, it's the best you've got." In doing so you will find that as a woman you are a lot stronger than you ever realized. Somehow you live through the unendurable and reach out for the impossible. It's a woman's own special survival mystique.

Letters I wish I'd mailed
  to the man who divorced me
    to marry a waitress

Dear Andrew,

Groundhog Day was always my favorite fun holiday.
Why did you have to pick this month to finalize the divorce?
I will never be able to enjoy February again. During lunch
at school today, I was paged for a phone call. My lawyer
told me that the divorce was final. I remember returning
to the table but I don't remember the meal. I kept thinking
to myself. "I'm divorced. I'm divorced." It still didn't make
any sense.

It made even less sense for us to have dinner together
so that the world would know that we were civilized adults.
All through the meal I kept thinking that I was divorced
but I didn't feel any different. I'm afraid to think what the
children thought when we came home and went up to our
bedroom. How strange to not be married and make love to
the man who had only a few hours earlier been your husband. Sometimes I think I will lose my mind. Sometimes
I believe I have already lost it. I couldn't turn my thoughts
off after you left. Sleep was out of reach. How do you
resolve the words: "Whosoever God has joined together, let
no man put asunder?" In my heart I am still your wife,
and you are still my husband. Why are you doing this to
me and to the children and to yourself? I need you, they
need you, and I think you need us.

I must be insane to be divorced from you at noon and
to make love with you in the evening. I don't have any pride.
I don't have any strength. I only have this feeble hope that
it is all a terrible mistake and that once you have experienced divorce, you will come home. We need you so very

1

much. I need you so very much. I wouldn't let you come back but I believe and the doctor believes that you must still love me or you wouldn't want me physically. I hope the doctor and I are right. I hope I am right. I don't think I can take much more. I have this terrible pain as if someone has physically ripped out my living heart. I know it is only my thoughts and my emotions, but the pain seems real. Oh, Andrew, how can you love me one minute and walk out of my life the next?

All my love always,
Adrianne

February 8, 1972

My dear Andrew,

Leslie cried this evening over the divorce. It was the most that she had cried since this all started. Scott and I tried everything to make her stop crying. Scott began to tell her all the good things about not having you around on a full-time basis. He finally made her laugh when he told her she would never again have to pick up her shoes. You always got upset because she would come in and promptly take off her shoes and leave them in the middle of the floor. If we didn't keep after her, she would continue to do this until she would have three or four pairs of shoes in various parts of the living room. Scott told her that now she could put all her shoes in the middle of the living room floor, and no one would say a word.

He also explained that never again would she have to vacuum under the cushions of the davenport. You must have been the only father in the world who checked whether the kids did their sweeping by looking under the cushions of the davenport. Little did you know that some weeks when they were in a hurry they would only sweep under the cushions and never do the floor. That used to be our private joke.

Scott and I also promised Leslie that she could stay on

2

the phone as long as she wanted and no one would say: "Leslie Ann, I am expecting a call!" We also told her that she could go for a week without making her bed if she wanted. After she thought about it for awhile she felt better. At least she stopped crying, and soon we were all trying to make bad jokes to cheer each other up. There is something about a really bad joke that makes everyone feel better.

When Leslie cries, I come as near to hating you as I am capable. I can take the pain for myself and for Scott, but somehow when I think of how you have hurt her, it is difficult to be understanding. When a daughter is sixteen, she shouldn't be in the middle of a parent's divorce. The only thing that keeps me from wanting to destroy you completely is the fact that maybe in time we will be able to work this out so that we will once again be a family. I believe that being a family is the most important concept in the world. I guess I will never be able to face the fact that this marriage is over.

All my love always,
Adrianne

February 12, 1972

Dear Andrew,

I turned on the faucet in the kitchen and nothing happened. I turned on the faucet in the bathroom and there was water. I know it is twelve below zero outside, but nothing like this ever happened when you were home. I felt the pipes under the sink and they were cold. Nothing seemed to be leaking, so I tried to call you. You are supposed to be here when I need you. What do I know about pipes that are frozen? Why didn't they freeze when I was married to you? Everything is colder without you.

Finally, I decided that doing something was better than standing in the middle of the kitchen crying. So I got my hair dryer and hooked it up with an extension cord and focused the warm air on the pipes under the sink. I left the

3

faucets open and soon there was a faint dripping sound. It wasn't long until the water started to run at a normal rate. I am probably the first plumber in history to use a hair dryer to solve a plumbing problem. I know you would laugh at me but it worked. I wish you were here to laugh at me. I miss you so very much.

It isn't the same when we have dinner together at a restaurant. The magic isn't there. We touch but I am too numb to feel it. It's a cat and mouse game, and I don't know if I'm the cat or the mouse. Maybe I'm the trap. Does it matter? Does anything matter? I'm putting the electric light under the cabinet so there will be some heat under the sink. I couldn't fight a broken pipe along with everything else. I hope the kids don't get tangled up in the cord and electrically fry themselves. If you were here, I know you would figure out some logical and safe way of doing this. I'm not logical or safe or anything else that makes sense. I'm just lonely for what no longer exists. I can thaw out a frozen pipe. Will I be able to thaw out your frozen heart?

All my love always,
Adrianne

February 14, 1972

Andrew,

I can't stop crying. What a hell of a way to spend Valentine's Day! I'm shaking, I'm still afraid, and worst of all—you don't care! Your only son totally destroyed his car and by some miracle walked away without a scratch, and you don't even care. It was written all over your face. You were more concerned over what it would cost you to replace the car than what you might have lost as a son. When I saw the car on its top, all crushed down, I couldn't believe that it had actually been Scott who had called me. Then I saw Scott standing there in that ridiculous overcoat with glass all over his head and shoulders. Yes, I cried. Yes, I was

4

hysterical. Yes, I embarrassed you. No, I'm not sorry. It was my female way of letting the world know that I was thankful to have a living son and a dead car and not the other way around.

Maybe I'm too hard on you. I should be thankful that you got there to help. I was in no condition to handle anything. At least you got us to the doctor. We made sure that our son was not injured in any way. I suppose I should appreciate the tranquilizers but they frighten me. It would be too easy on a night like this to take the whole bottle of them.

I need you here with me tonight. This is the kind of night that needs a marriage. A husband and wife should be helping each other. Instead, this is just one more nightmare in which I am alone. I hear every tick of the clock, every squeak and crunch of the house, and most of all I hear the nothingness and the emptiness. I can't stop crying. The tears just keep welling up. I don't know if I am crying for my son, the accident, my broken marriage, my broken life, or because I don't know what else to do. Why can't I properly hate you? "One door never closes unless another opens." "This too shall pass." "Laugh, and the world laughs with you; cry, and you cry alone." All the standard phrases of comfort, and only one seems to fit: "Cry, and you cry alone." Please come back. I can't make it alone.

All my love always,
Adrianne

P.S. You didn't send me a Valentine!

February 20, 1972
Dear Andrew,
Leslie brought home this long-haired case of terminal acne and introduced him as her date. I wanted to vomit because he couldn't keep his hands off her while they were

just standing there. If you were here you could have killed him. Fathers are supposed to do things like that. Mothers have to be polite even if it kills them on the inside. I've read enough books to know that this is Leslie's way of reacting toward the divorce. If I cause a scene, she will cause a bigger one, and I know that isn't the answer.

I know that I have to be cool. I may be crumbling away on the inside but I have to be cool when we talk about Mr. Wonderful. I know she will be watching my reaction. If she knows I hate the sight of him, she is bound to fall in love with him. They are downstairs shooting pool. As long as I hear the pool balls hitting each other, I won't worry. You should be here. Leslie is your daughter. Do you want this for a son-in-law? Why don't you answer the phone when I really need you? If there isn't anyone else in your life, where do you spend so much time? Oh, my God, I don't hear the pool balls. I don't hear anything. He is so bad she could get leprosy, V.D., or hoof-and-mouth disease just by touching him. Should I go downstairs? Andrew, why aren't you here to help me? Thank God! They are shooting pool again. This evening has got to end! Something has got to end! Will it be I?

Longingly,
Adrianne

February 22, 1972

Dear Andrew,

Tonight was a night that we should have been together. It was ridiculous for you to be in one row and for me to be in another. That was our son on the stage giving his first high-school performance as an actor. His timing as a comedian was excellent. We should have been together sharing his excitement. I couldn't believe that Scott could step into the male lead of *Matchmaker* on two week's notice and do so well. He is a very talented young man, and I am bursting with parental pride.

6

Oh, Andrew, when we can be responsible for bringing two such wonderful children into the world, do we have the right to give up now? I don't think we do. They are almost grown but the children need us as parents, not as two people worlds apart.

I was glad that you came over to the house after the play. I wanted to share the pride of being a parent. I wanted to talk about all the things Scott had done that were great. I thought this was what you would want to share. I couldn't believe what you had in mind. I tried to please you but my heart was not in it. I am not a prude but your desires upset me. I tried to please you but my heart was not in it. Sex has to be more than gymnastics. Where is the tenderness? Where is the sharing and the understanding? Inside I know that I love you. I have loved you for so long I can't stop. Yet, I must not love you enough because I can't cope with your new and strange sexual idiosyncrasies. I try to pretend but inside I know that I'm revolted, and I know you sense my aversion and hate me for having it. I know my attitude upsets you but I still wish you would at least talk to our family doctor. There is something wrong. You are not the man I have known through the years. How will I be able to live with your new desires? I am ready to give up. Then I think of our son and of our daughter, and I know that I must try harder. Our family is too important to be destroyed. I must hold us together.

Please know that I love you,
Adrianne

February 28, 1972

Dear Andrew,

For a short month, February has been the longest month I have ever lived through. I am in the classroom every day, but I have no idea what I am teaching. Leslie and Scott are both gone this evening. I hear house noises that I have never heard before. I am certain that someone is dying in the attic but I am not about to find out for sure. I haven't heard from you for several days. I want to call you but I can't. I guess I am afraid that you won't be there. I can't help but wonder what you do with your extra time.

Your parents came up on Sunday, and it was very awkward. After all the times we have spent together, we suddenly have nothing to say. I guess I can't forgive your mother for believing that I should give you a divorce. She said that if I gave you a divorce, someday you would thank me for it. I can't help but think that was a really freaky thing for one woman to tell another. To think I will not have you but your eternal gratitude. That does not keep me warm in a king-size bed.

I keep thinking that you must have a brain tumor or some disease that is upsetting your brain cells. I simply cannot accept the fact that after all these years you simply stopped loving me. It doesn't make sense. There has to be something more than meets the eye. I am so lonely this evening that I don't think I can take it. I find myself wishing I were dead. Somehow there is something comforting in the thought of being dead. It is so final and so efficient. The body is buried and out of the way. It's not that way with a divorce. It doesn't end, it just hurts. I keep waking up at three o'clock in the morning, and for the first time in my life, I am afraid. This is a new experience for me, and I hate it. I need you to tell me that some way, somehow, we will work this out. It doesn't happen. I have to work this out by myself.

Divorce is bad enough but the little things are closing in on me. This day has been a disaster. Scott yelled that the toilet was overflowing again and I stepped in the dog shit on the way to help him. He had driven my car last night and brought it back registering empty, so I was nearly late to school. The students were nightmares, and when I got home Leslie had burnt the spaghetti sauce, and my favorite pan will never be the same. As I walked through the house, I noticed that the light bulbs were taking turns burning out.

I should try to accept these things as ways of keeping my mind off you, but believe me, they don't help. I think the worst part of all was sitting on the recently cracked toilet seat and getting my butt pinched. At least you could come over and fix that. Nothing is going right without you. Please come back.

All my love,
Adrianne

March 3, 1972

Dear Andrew,

It is two in the morning, and I can't go back to sleep. You have got to do something about Scott's car. I cannot cope with this situation. I know that you have taken it into the filling station, but you will have to take it back and yell at them. I had taken a tranquilizer and gone to bed because I could not stand the sound of the rain. Too much of our lives was surrounded by rain. Our first date was a picnic in the rain, we were married on a rainy day, we walked in the rain, and every one of those raindrops tonight said: "Remember Andrew." I shut it out and went to sleep and the phone rang.

Scott had taken his date to Burger Spot after the show and when he tried to start the car, it wouldn't start. So there was no one to help, and he didn't have the money to call a service station. So he called me. I had to dress and drive up there in the rain. I pulled up and parked next to him and immediately Rent-a-Cop, the friendly policeman who patrols, came up to tell me not to loiter. I had to explain that my son's car wouldn't start and that I was going to try to use the battery jumpers.

I was scared to death because of the rain but I got the hood open and the cables out and figured Scott would know how to hook them up to the battery terminals. Wrong! That's what I get for having a bookworm for a son. He didn't know his negative from his positive, so I had to rely on memory from the times I had helped you. Rent-a-Cop just stood there picking his nose. I got them hooked up, and I didn't electrocute myself but I was terrified. About that time, Rent-a-Cop drawls out: "Ya know, not many women would know how to do that." Had I said I did? The days of chivalry are dead. Male chauvinist pigs, where are you?

The car started but by then I was soaked, and I had to follow Scott to Jamie's house. Then he kissed her good-night and I got to follow him back home. He had a loving evening, and I am reduced to writing you my sad tales of woe. Why aren't you here to kiss me goodnight or jump my battery or jump me or do something? I'll never get back to sleep, and I have tests to give tomorrow.

Andrew, I don't like being a woman alone. Yes, I solve the problems but it is no fun to do it alone.

All my love,
Adrianne

March 7, 1972

Dear Andrew,

Thank you for coming over and putting the new seat on the toilet. I don't mind a friendly pinch but that toilet was getting out of hand. It was like being a family again when I came home and found you working in the bathroom and the kids starting supper. If I had known you were coming over I could have planned something more exciting than beef and noodles. You did seem to enjoy the home cooking, even if it was left over from Sunday.

Leslie was smiling more than I had seen her smile in a long time. She misses you more than you realize. Going bowling or to the restaurant isn't like being together as a family. Leslie hates it when you come after her and Scott to go out to eat. It is such an artificial situation. Oh, Andrew, how can you spend the evening with us and then leave?

After the children went upstairs to study and we built

a fire in the fireplace, it was so nice. Sometimes when you smile at me, I think that if I hang on a little while longer it will work out. I hope so. We have so many things going for us as a family. It would be wrong to give up now. I have trouble accepting your idea of liberated sex, but I am trying. The doctor says to make you happy, but it frightens me. You have changed, and I am not sure this change is normal. I am trying to understand and to cooperate if it means saving our marriage. Most of the evening was good. That's what I will try to remember.

All my love,
Adrianne

March 9, 1972
Dear Andrew,

Schools are impossible. I don't care if I am a teacher, there are times I cannot go along with the Mickey Mouse shit they hand out. Scott has missed more days of school than he has attended all during his life. Why, during the senior year when he comes in and aces the tests and is geared to be a valedictorian, do they decide to come on with a heavy rule that if he misses fifteen days he loses his credits? There is no way that I will hold still for that. I can produce a doctor's excuse for the times that he has missed. An arbitrary rule like that is ridiculous.

Eastside High School should be embarrassed that a student can miss that much time and walk into the class and get an A. That seems to be some kind of commentary on either his ability or their lack of challenge as teachers. I left my school and told the assistant principal of Eastside, a Mr. Denver, in no uncertain terms that if they decided to push the issue I would take it as far as I had to in order to keep Scott's credits. I don't think their rule is legal according to state regulations. Anyway, I told them I would start with the school board and go on to the state department of public instruction. I think they got the message

11

because all of a sudden Mr. Denver was willing to accept the doctor's excuses.

That's what is rotten about education. If the parents care enough to go in and scream long enough and loud enough, they can get anything changed, altered, or amended. I always feel sorry for the kid who gets the shaft from the system because he doesn't have anyone to yell and to threaten for him. Equal education is far from being equal.

I do appreciate the fact that you reinforced my comments. Scott said he has not had any further problems. Somehow the future valedictorian of a class shouldn't lose his credits, or the Eastside teachers might all wind up being embarrassed. Maybe I should rant and rave more often. Somehow I feel a little perkier.

Love,
Adrianne

March 14, 1972

Dear Andrew,

I am truly sorry that I couldn't drink the martini. I know it is a small thing, but I didn't like the taste of it. I ordered it because I thought you would be more comfortable if I ordered a drink. I thought I could drink it but it tasted like perfume and I couldn't get it down. I did not mean to cause a national incident. I will mail you the dollar and thirty-five cents. I think it is permissible to waste a martini without feeling guilty about the starving children of Biafra. I did not need an economy lecture. My whole way of life is destroyed, and you become hyper about a wasted martini. I don't think I am capable of understanding the divorced male.

I can't help but point out to you that I didn't smoke and I didn't drink when we discussed getting married, and I never did during the eighteen years of our marriage. Let's face it, I am not going to make it as a smoker and a drinker. It really shouldn't matter. I don't care if you smoke or have

12

a drink so why should it bother you if I drink a Coke? I try, but I can't be something I am not.

Andrew, try to meet me part of the way. I want you to be you and to be free and comfortable and happy. Can't you let me be me? Why can't we simply be a family again? Why do I have to be a sophisticated whore? I am sorry but that is what you act like you want me to be. I have done things that I have never even read about, and I cannot believe that this type of living pornography is what marriage means. I wish you would see a doctor or a psychiatrist or whatever it takes to get things back together. I will see one too if you think it will help. Let's get some kind of help because this is not the answer.

My love for you and for the children is too great to give up now. There has to be an answer, and some way we will find it.

All my love,
Adrianne

P.S.   I did eat the olive! Doesn't that count?

March 16, 1972

Dear Andrew,

Leslie has said farewell to Mr. Wonderful forever. There is no way that I can express my relief. I knew that if I kept my mouth shut, that her natural good taste would come through. They only had a few dates but I worried myself to pieces. He never stopped touching her. I don't know how she ever fought him off in private. Anyway I am thankful that he is out of the picture. Now she is talking about a young man named Mark, and he sounds much better. Actually, after Mr. Wonderful, the neighborhood vampire would be an improvement.

I hope that Mark Hamilton really is as nice as he sounds. Leslie misses you so much that she needs something good in her life. People need love in their lives, and if they don't find it in one place, they look in another. I hope that she doesn't get too serious too fast. A boyfriend and an early marriage would be the worst thing that could happen to her right now. Leslie needs time to adjust before she does anything that is serious enough to change her whole future.

God, I must be nuts. Leslie hasn't even brought him home, and I have her planning a wedding. That is one thing I hate most about your leaving. For some reason I don't understand, even my smallest fear becomes magnified. I spend hours worrying about the most trivial things. By now I should realize that nothing really matters. There is a time limit on everything, and the limit is beyond our individual control.

People tell me that one of these days I will meet someone. I don't want to meet anyone. I never want to care this much about a human being again. Besides there could never be anyone to replace you in any way.

Love,
Adrianne

P.S.   Remember our first date?

March 17, 1972

Dear Andrew,

Happy St. Patrick's Day and may you turn green all over your body. I get so weary of your constant picking. If you want to make noises like a father and a husband, come home and do it. Otherwise, you will have to accept things the way they are. There is no way that I plan to be both mother and father to two teenagers. Believe me, being a mother is tricky enough. Long hair for Scott is not the end of the world. I know he hasn't had a haircut since you left. Yes, I will agree that he is beginning to look like Cousin It from the TV show. I am mildly sorry that your circle of friends still associate boys who have long hair with either fairies or hippies. To which do you object, the fairies or the hippies? At this point, I don't think he is either. If, however, you keep issuing ultimatums and harassing him, I can't guarantee anything.

Try to understand that long hair on a boy for this generation is entirely different. It simply means that he is asserting himself as an individual. Try to look at it from my viewpoint. I'm putting up not only with long hair but long hair that is curlier and prettier than mine. That really hurts. Why do you suddenly have all these hang-ups about what people will think? You don't seem to care what people think about your divorcing me. That seems a lot more serious than the length of our son's hair.

For a man who works with young people, you have a lot of screwed-up ideas. I don't see why you can't accept the fact that teenagers in each generation have to be unique and original. In growing up, they look for an identity that is different from their parents. For a little while I looked through the picture album of when we were dating. There was a picture of you with long hair but it was slicked back into a high pompadour. You had super-wide padded shoulders in your sport coat, and baggy pants with cuffs. To top it off and make you fantastic, you were wearing a pair of white buck shoes. That was the code for a man-about-town when we were young. I can't see that Scott's hair looks any more weird than yours did in the picture. Your hair was appropriate for your generation, and his is appropriate for his generation.

I am sorry to disappoint you but I will not insist that he cut his hair. When he is ready to cut it, he will. Until then, I'll look at the person under the hair. You know, Andrew, it is possible to love a person without expecting the impossible.

Scott is my son, and without you here, he is my responsibility. I give him the right to be an individual. No, he doesn't put his hair up on rollers. Why do we have to be so far apart on everything? There was a time when we were so close about everything. Come back before it is too late.

Love,
Adrianne

March 20, 1972

Dear Andrew,

You just missed a moment of happiness. Leslie came in from a date with Mark. She was floating to a music all her own. She couldn't wait to tell me that Mark had asked her to go steady. Sixteen and going steady are a dream come true. This is the happiest that she has been for a very long time. I imagine that this will probably be the first of many times that she will come in and tell me that she is going steady. She needs to date a variety of fellows before she becomes too serious about any one young man. I wonder if I had dated more fellows if I would have known how to be a better and more exciting person. I know that I did something wrong along the way or we would still be together.

Mark is a nice person. He is quiet most of the time but he has a sense of humor and that helps. He drives an old pickup truck. He has already offered to help us with the moving. I am glad that Leslie has someone special that she can relate to. I know that most of the time I am not much help.

You and I used to laugh and say that love was like a warm candle in my tummy. Now I feel like someone has blown out the candle and all that is left is cold emptiness. Sharing Leslie's happiness with her brought back memories of my own. I will never forget the night you pinned your fraternity pin on my blouse. I should have stuffed it up your left nostril and run like hell. No, I can't wish away the years we shared. There were too many good times, especially the children. I just hope Leslie moves like a snail in her new relationship. I think it is important that she go

16

slowly in developing a new friendship. Right now she is so vulnerable. I want her to take her time and to enjoy the luxury of being young. Most of us have to grow up too soon.

All my love always,
Adrianne

March 24, 1972

Oh God, Andrew,

How could you? I can't believe that you would do this to me and to the children. There has to be some terrible mistake. It has to be a hoax. There is no way I can believe this. The phone rang and Leslie answered on the extension and said it was for me. Before she could hang up on her phone, someone said, "Adrianne, I thought you would like to know that Andrew is getting married this evening." When I asked who the woman was, she hung up. Then I heard Leslie crying because she didn't have any idea that you would see me one week and get married the next. There was nothing I could say to her that would ease the pain. We could only put our arms around each other and cry until there were no tears left for either for us. There were no words to help us now.

I knew that you had started seeing someone, but this is ridiculous. How could you—my husband, the father of my children, an elementary school principal—how could you marry a waitress? It couldn't be that waitress! You said that you hardly knew her. This cannot be happening. Surely you would tell me. You couldn't date me one minute and marry someone else the next. I think I am going to throw up. I thought Leslie would never stop crying. This time the jokes did not help. I tried to laugh about it and say it was a joke, but a call like this could not have been a joke. This is the start of spring vacation for the schools. There is no way that I can even find out if this is true until later. There isn't anyone I can call. How do I call someone and say, "Oh, by the way, do you happen to know if my

17

former husband got married this evening?" I keep hoping that it was a wrong number, but they called me by name.

Oh, my God, when I think of what I have tried to do to keep us together. I can't believe that you would treat me in this way. You couldn't make love to me last week and marry her this week and be sane. If you are sane, after what I have submitted to, then there is no hope for me. If you are sane and normal then I have no hope for myself.

Even if I could forgive you for what you have done to me, how could I ever forget the look on Leslie's face or the tears that would not stop? Andrew, you have done a rotten thing, and tonight I don't love you.

Damn you,
Adrianne

P.S. If this is true, I hope your new wife's legs grow together.

March 31, 1972

Dear Son of a Bitch,

In all the years that we were married I never called you names or swore at you. Now I cannot think of anything rotten enough to adequately describe you. School is back in session, and everyone knows that you married a waitress from Fort Brad. The shame! The embarrassment! The nausea! Any other man your age who left his wife would at least go out and marry some cute little blonde half his age. But you, you have to marry a thirty-five-year-old pudgy waitress with a ridiculous bouffant hairstyle and two children.

There is no way in this world, after hearing this, that I will believe that you are a sane and rational person. You are sick! You are demented! You are possessed! There is something about this whole situation that I cannot understand. If I ever put all the pieces together I may shoot both of you.

The worst part of this is knowing that in my heart I still love you. You are my husband, the father of my children, and the first man I ever loved. I know that I can't turn my love off. I hate what you have done to me and to the children, but love doesn't end. It is there, and I am trying to understand how my love lasts and yours is revitalized for a frowzy waitress.

I know that I will never again leave a tip for a waitress. From now on, waitresses are my enemies. You are my enemy! I will stop loving you. It will take time but I will stop. When I learn to hate you with a vengeance, I will be free. Until then—go to hell, Andrew!

Angrily,
Adrianne

April 2, 1972

Dear Andrew,

Today all two hundred and fifty pounds of my angry mother arrived. She will never be satisfied until she has the opportunity to step on your head. I really have mixed emotions. I know it would not do any good for the two of you to have a conversation, but she gets very persistent. Even though I know it would not accomplish anything for you and mother to meet, I sometimes get a lot of pleasure out of thinking what might happen. I can see her rushing toward you, tripping, and flattening you. There is, at times, a certain amount of pure pleasure in thinking about you in a situation that would bring you great physical pain and agony. Certainly two hundred and fifty pounds of hurtling flab could accomplish that.

I realize now that I should have listened to her when she suggested that I hire a private detective to check on your activities in Fort Brad when you were supposed to be so busy with the Indiana Air National Guard. How was I to know that you were spending your time tipping a waitress? Most men are content to leave a quarter under the coffee cup, but you had to leave your shoes under her bed. It is difficult to listen to my mother telling me her favorite words: "I told you so!" Why did I have to have faith in you? I know now why the wife is the last to know. She is the last to give in and listen to the truth.

There is no point in writing this evening. I need all my strength to talk mother out of firebombing your car. She alternates between that and running over you with her Nova. She is obsessed with waiting for you to come out of school and then running over you. Her face really lights up when she talks about leaping out of the car and seeing you lying there with the tire on your chest. Then she wants to tell you that it was wrong to divorce me. I keep telling her that at that point you probably wouldn't want to listen.

If I ever decide to encourage her, I like what she has in mind for Peg. We have been told that Peg has a super-bouffant hairstyle. The thought of mother sitting on Peg's chest while she plucks her head bald gives me a certain amount of sadistic pleasure. Maybe I shouldn't discourage mother from a little good clean fun.

Love,
Adrianne

April 4, 1972

Dear Andrew,

We have barely been divorced two months and your new wife has to publicly embarrass all of us. Why in the name of heaven would the wife of an elementary school principal send a letter to the editor of the local paper saying she was in favor of homosexuals? Now I admit that I did some unusual things as your wife, but this is insane. Peg not only sent it, she signed it with her full name and address.

The children and I have tried to make light of it by saying that she is probably advertising, but it really isn't funny. This town is too small to accept that type of opinion from the wife of an elementary school principal. Is she trying to destroy your reputation or create one for herself? Isn't she aware of the scandal a few years ago that involved one of the elementary principals for that very problem? I wonder if you knew about the letter before it came out in the paper? I can only hope that you didn't.

Maybe if it came as a surprise to you, you might go home and beat hell out of her. In that case I would feel that the letter was an excellent idea. May she write many more. I guess I should be glad that she gave her name instead of saying Mrs. Andrew H. Helman. I guess I could have been blamed for it and that would have been awkward.

I know one thing, when I go to school tomorrow the first thing I plan to do is to write my full name on the chalkboard so that there is absolutely no doubt about my identity. I can't help but wish that the letter would provide grounds for divorce, but I doubt it. Maybe Peg is a pervert in disguise. It does make me wonder about several things. But those are things to which I don't really want to know the answers. I don't want answers, I want action. Go home and divorce her and come back to the ones who really love you. I miss you so very much.

Love,
Adrianne

April 6, 1972

Dear Andrew,

When you offered to attend the meeting at Eastside High School with Scott I thought it was an excellent idea. I still have the confused idea that you and I need to act as the units of a family whenever possible. The children need you as a father. I thought it would be a rewarding experience for you and for Scott to be together when the various colleges were going to be at the high school to discuss their programs and scholarships.

The phone call from you at eleven this evening was totally unexpected. I can't believe that you, as the principal of an integrated school, would react in that manner. Swearing at me because your son walked into the high school with a black girl does not make sense. You blew your cool. You regressed a hundred years and saw your son walk in with a "nigger." You were afraid of what your friends might say. Isn't it sad that your son thought that he had walked in with a friend who needed a ride? Remember, we taught him to look at the person and not at the color. How can you and he be a world apart in your values?

I can't believe that because Scott offered Marie a ride and walked in with her that he is going to marry her and, to quote you, raise little "high yeller pickaninnies." Your super-bigoted attitude made me ill. We taught him to walk the half mile to help a fellow human being. Now, when he is living the values we gave him, you are upset. I am sorry, but I am proud of him.

I did not appreciate your yelling and swearing at me over the phone. For a man who never swore during our married life, you have developed some vocabulary. Try to remember that our son is an individual and that he has the freedom to live his life. If that includes a black girl, a yellow girl, or a green girl, it will be his choice, and I will not love him any less. I'm not upset by his actions. I am upset by your attitude. If a highly educated man like yourself can be democratic enough to marry a waitress, surely you could be tolerant of your son. I don't see how you could change so quickly. What has happened to your values and beliefs?

It hurts me to think you were afraid someone saw your son walk in with a black girl. I didn't swear back at you tonight, but neither did I miss you quite so much.

Less love,
Adrianne

P.S. You get one laugh. Scott took Marie home, and the goddamn car wouldn't start. So I had to go to the corner of 8th and Hackley—yes, the heart of the black section—

22

to jump his car battery. I'm sorry to report I was neither mugged nor raped! Yes, sir, Mister Principal, Whitey made it into enemy territory and back without a racial incident.

April 10, 1972

Dear Andrew,

The children had supper with you at the Big Whiz Restaurant. When they came back, they were both upset. Leslie and Scott need you as a father and they miss you. Because they love you very much, they don't want to hurt you. But you are pushing them too fast. It is too soon to expect them to meet your new wife. Andrew, you are giving them too many changes too rapidly. You destroyed us as a family, are you determined to destroy us as individuals?

Why can't you give them time to adjust? Why do you feel that you can do no wrong and that everyone else must accept and approve of you! Doesn't it seem a little strange that you could put your wedding date on the school calendar ahead of time, but not say anything to the children and me? Have you forgotten that you never did tell your daughter about your marriage? That Leslie heard it from an anonymous phone call? Remember, they see Peg as part of what destroyed the security they had lived with all their lives. I am sorry I am a mess, but they see it. I can't roll with this experience. It is slowly destroying me. When Leslie and Scott know that I am crying and unhappy, they are not going to rush into Peg's arms with love. It doesn't work that way. Give us a decent time allowance to bury this dead marriage.

If you don't push them, I am sure that they will come around. In a few months you can invite them over for a home-cooked meal. I'll even give them some change so they can leave a tip for your new wife. That ought to make her feel right where she belongs. Right now the children need love, patience, and understanding from both of us. They are afraid to meet her. After all, they could pick up a bad case of dishpan hands. It will be a disaster if you push them.

Love,
Adrianne

April 11, 1972

Dear Andrew,

Tonight I am truly frightened. Scott has been keeping very late hours and his whole circle of friends has changed. This evening he brought in three guys who really disturb me. It isn't their size or their manner, but what they seem to represent. They have such big wide pupils in their eyes, and they just seem to float in, loving everybody and everything. The strange, sweet sickening odor that permeates their clothing is what I fear most.

Scott asked if they could spend the night, and I have never turned any of his friends away but I wanted to turn them away. They represent an element that we don't need to be involved with at this time. Divorce is bad enough without all the side effects. The boys were upstairs with the stereo blasting strange electronic sounds when I decided to hang up their coats. When I picked up the one leather jacket, a metal film container dropped out. When I lifted it, something inside shifted, and I knew it wasn't film. I opened it, and it was grass. I closed the lid quickly and put it back in the jacket and put the jacket back on the pool table. There is no way I can play a heavy scene.

If I call you, I know you would probably call the police, and I am not about to be busted in a drug raid. I could make them get out, but I am afraid that with the tension from the divorce Scott would go with them. I don't think that he is smoking grass but I do think that he is testing me. He believes that you don't love any of us, and he is testing to see if I love him enough to put up with his new choice of friends. After the scene you made about Marie, he doesn't trust us as parents. He is questioning our values and beliefs. Scott thinks we talk one set and live

24

another. I have to help him understand that I tell it and live it like it is.

Right now there are a thousand thoughts running through my mind and none of them make any sense. Maybe I should just roll me a reefer and join them. It might be nice to drift off into a fantasy world where I could love everyone and everyone would love me. But then, I spent eighteen years in one. The fantasy world is fine, it's the waking up that hurts. I don't imagine drugs would be any more kind.

The music is still vibrating throughout the house. My nerves are like raw sores. The harder I try to think, the more it hurts. I don't need drugs to experience a bad trip. I am on one and it only gets worse. A confrontation with Scott while the other boys are here is not the answer. Somehow I will have faith in the fact that he is my son. He is too intelligent to mess up his mind and his world. Scott is fighting the pain of divorce in his way. He is reaching out for new experiences. At the same time, he is testing us. He too wants to know if love ends. You showed him that it does. I have to show him that it lasts. I won't turn his friends out. I'll just pray that I don't get busted.

Love,
Adrianne

April 12, 1972

Dear Andrew,

Leslie has gained thirty pounds. She cannot cope with seeing you for an evening meal and hearing you talk only about how much Peg wants to meet her. Can't you simply be Leslie's father when you are with her? She needs to know that she is important and that she is loved as your only daughter. Is it impossible for you to put someone else's feelings ahead of your own?

Right now Leslie doesn't have any desire to meet Peg.

After you brought Leslie home this evening, she made the statement that if you could stop loving me and divorce me, then she could stop loving you and divorce you as a father. It is very difficult for me to explain to her that you will not stop loving her as a daughter when she knows that you are capable of putting time limits on your love. I won't say anything to make her hate you, but how can I make you see while you are not doing or saying anything to make her love you or show her that you love her.

For a man who got A's in child psychology, you are surely getting an F in practicing it. Please stop frustrating Leslie or I will make a sandwich board that says "Andrew H. Helman Is a Dropout Father." Then I will picket your school wearing it.

Love,
Adrianne

April 13, 1972

Dear Andrew,

Today I faced the fact that the children and I will be moving back to our rental property. I will not miss cleaning three toilet bowls. I will miss the woods in back, the sound of the birds, the spaciousness, the fireplace, and the rare moments of happiness that we shared as a family. This was never my home, this was a place I visited. I knew when we looked at this house that it would never be my home. I knew we would buy it but I would not live here long. I am sorry now that I didn't insist that we use the money we inherited to take us as a family to Europe. Memories of a family trip to Europe would have always been good. I wonder why I always know the ending when something begins.

Home will be Palmer Court, and I don't mind going back to a house that holds the memories of our married life. It represents the happiness we shared, and I will be comfortable there. Our children grew up there, and I know Leslie will feel more secure in our old home rather than in an apartment. For Scott, it doesn't matter—he is cutting the umbilical cord with great haste and finality. Divorce gave him his adulthood in a hurry.

Now I must pick and choose. How will I make myself do the things that must be done? I find myself lying perfectly still and staring at a crack in the ceiling. There are things to be done and decisions to be made, and I waste hours staring at the same spot. When the children leave, I lie down and stare at the space. I don't move, I don't cry, I don't think, I just exist. Eternity stretches ahead of me, and I only see the crack on the ceiling. I'm not asleep. I'm not awake. I'm just in this spot wishing everything would end. Somehow the crack is comforting because it doesn't change. There is a security in knowing that it stays the same. People are very kind and very understanding but they don't seem to realize that there is no longer any significance in anything for me. I don't understand what has happened, and because I don't, I can't go on. There is no way I can function in this situation. It is terrible for the children. They know I am afraid to be alone. I am afraid of what I may do. Everything that I believed in has ended. When you took your love away, you took the marriage, the ideals, the values, and my identity. For as many years as I can remember, I have been Andrew's wife. Now I'm not Andrew's wife, and I don't know who I am. I lived a certain way. I reacted a certain way. I believed in certain values. These are all gone and I'm lost. I have the children for a time. I have teaching. Something inside says, hang on, but it becomes weaker and I must lie very still to hear it at all. It would be so much easier to let go. I've never been a quitter, but then I've never before been divorced.

Softly,
Adrianne

April 17, 1972

Dear Andrew,

The little things are really getting to me. Every time I forget to shut my bedroom door or the children forget to shut it, I come home to the same old problem. One of the dachshunds keeps hiking in the middle of my king size bed. Three times this week I have come home to a wet stained bedspread. They never did this when you were home. I can't understand why it is happening now. It is hard to concentrate on teaching English when you have visions of a small dachshund stealthily creeping through the hall to see if my bedroom door is open. The little dog looks furtively around to see that no one is in sight. Then he runs at full speed and jumps onto the bed. He deliberately hikes in the center of the bedspread. I can see him saunter to the edge and jump off feeling that he has shown me. If I ever find out which one is doing it, we will have barbecued dog.

It wouldn't be so bad if I could toss the spread in the washer but I have to toss the sheets in the washer and then take the bedspread out to the do-it-yourself dry cleaners. The matron out there is beginning to think that I am a call girl or some kind of cleanliness freak because I keep cleaning the same bedspread. There is no way that I will try to explain to her what is really happening. I guess I will have to start locking the bedroom door. I think the kids are leaving it open after they go in to use the extension phone. I can think of better ways to mess up a bedspread but those days are gone forever. If you want custody of the dogs, call me. I don't need them. I only need you.

Love,
Adrianne

April 19, 1972

Happy Anniversary, Andrew,

Will you make love to your waitress on this, our very special night? Nineteen years ago was our wedding night.

28

I wonder if you will remember our first night of love. Somehow I'll remember the things we've done, the places we've gone, and the words we've spoken. I go over the years looking for clues. Where does a marriage begin to end? Where did you decide to stop loving me? Worst of all, did you ever love me? Suppose all those years were wasted for both of us? When I look back I can't find the answers. There are only more questions. Why can't I die and get it over?

Please, Andrew, remember me tonight. For just a little while, remember the love we shared. Let me believe that there is one regret for you, some small longing for what we shared. If I could believe that, I might be able to sleep. Regardless of what has happened, my love for you is deep within my heart. If you must make love to her tonight, at least call her by my name. Sleep well, my husband.

I love you,
Adrianne

April 21, 1972

Dear Andrew,

Your temper is showing in a very immature manner. The secretary from Dr. Rabenstein's office called to tell me in no uncertain terms that a Mr. Andrew H. Helman would not pay for Leslie's new prescription sunglasses. The secretary wanted to know if she could cancel the order. It took some soothing over on my part to calm her ruffled plumage. Your language over the phone had been very offensive. I assured her that the bill would be paid in full.

Sometimes I think that you are deliberately trying to create problems. I made a number of concessions concerning the divorce settlement with the understanding that we would be able to behave maturely and rationally in matters that concerned the children. You seem to have forgotten this part of the agreement. I do not want to fight you or to create problems, but you will have to accept your responsibilities toward the finances. There is no way that I can legally force you to love the children, but I will force you to pay the expenses.

In case you have forgotten, Leslie has worn tinted glasses since kindergarten. Sensitivity to light has always been one of her problems. Sunglasses have been routine since kindergarten. My lawyer, Mrs. McGill, understood this when I explained the situation. I thought Mrs. McGill phrased it well when she said, "Tell him he can either pay for the sunglasses now or pay for the sunglasses, lawyer's fees, and court costs later." She was correct in your reaction. You got the message so fast that it broke the connection on the phone.

Thank you for calling back two hours later. It was so romantic the way you said: "Adrianne, you've got me over a goddamn barrel so I'll pay for the sunglasses." You show genuine sportsmanship, especially if you have no other choice.

Forgive me for smiling but it was ridiculous. You can't be too happy in your new life or you wouldn't be so hyper. I won't make the bills difficult for you, but neither will I economize in any way that concerns the health and well-being of the children. I suppose when you get a dental bill (and you will get a dental bill soon) I will be blamed for feeding Leslie and Scott a steady diet of candy to rot out their teeth so you will have to pay to have them filled.

I can only say that talking to you on the phone is a psychedelic experience that I could forgo.

Love,
Adrianne

P.S. If you weren't a married man, I'd invite you over. I can think of a fantastic way to ease your tense situation. It would do me a world of good, too.

30

Dear Andrew,

The strangest things keep happening. Tonight the phone rang and it was Scott. He said that he was at the Literary Club and Angela was crying. Scott wanted me to talk to her and see if I could get her to stop crying. I'm near tears most of the time, and he wants me to comfort a girl I scarcely know over the telephone. Mothers sometimes do the impossible but this time it seemed like the ridiculous. All I could tell him was that I would try.

I told Scott to put Angela on the phone and I would see what I could do. He did and I heard this soft sobbing sound. Now, what do you say to a soft sob? So I called her by name and asked if she could tell me what was wrong. It seems that Angela is white and has a tendency to be attracted to young men of the black race. This creates a great many problems with her parents. She had been secretly dating one of the black guys named Bruce. One of Angela's neighbors, Mrs. Rockford, had seen them together and had told Angela's parents. Mrs. Rockford's daughter was at the Literary Club and had told Angela what her mother had done. Now Angela was afraid to go home.

Between sobs, Angela managed to pour out the whole story. I tried to be calm and rational but no matter how you play the scene it was going to be one hairy night when Angela got home to her Southern Baptist parents. All I could do was to tell her that she would have to go home and face it. Then I assured her that basically her parents loved her and wanted to do what was best for her. Angela would have to work with them to determine what was best for her. Getting angry and hysterical before she even got there was not going to help matters at all.

Then Angela asked if it would be acceptable to me if Scott took her home. Her parents like Scott, and she thought maybe they would not be so angry if he went along. I told her that would have to be Scott's decision. He is becoming

31

an expert on handling the big hairy scene with you, so I imagine he would be able to cope with Angela's parents.

Whether I did any good or not is debatable. At least by the time she said good-bye, she was no longer crying. I don't envy Scott taking her home, but I know he will because he tries to be there if a friend needs help. Oh, Andrew, where are you when I need help?

I wonder, if I would call and cry, would Peg let you come over and wipe away my tears? Someday I may take a chance and call.

All my love,
Adrianne

May 5, 1972

Andrew,

For your birthday I send you my deepest sympathy. Because it was your birthday, my thoughts were very much with you. I decided to start packing some of the things you had left in the closet. I thought it would be easier to do it on your birthday since there was no way to keep you out of my mind this afternoon. Needless to say, I burned the pornography. There is no way to explain the complete revulsion I felt when I started to find the books and pamphlets. I might have been able to accept the general tone of the material on the basis of male curiosity if it had not been for the photographs.

When I found the photographs, I knew it had to be more than mere curiosity on your part. No wonder I couldn't satisfy you—I was the wrong sex. At least I was the wrong sex part of the time. Why didn't you destroy this filth? Why did you leave it for me to find? Did you want me to know how sick you really are? What if one of the children had accidently found this stuff? Oh, Jesus, to think it was another principal that I should have been jealous of instead of the waitress.

I started to look through the stuff, and I couldn't. I

32

don't want to know what you became. I suppose that was Peg in the bouffant hairdo and nothing else. I have read about bi-sexual orgies but I never saw a picture of one before, and I hope with all my heart I never see one again. This explains more than I wanted to know.

These pictures could have ruined you as a principal and it would have ruined you as the father of my children. Someday I may be sorry that I did not keep the pictures as proof of how sick you really are. Instead, I am only thankful that I destroyed them. Now I will have to sort through everything. I can't take the chance that the children would find any of this trash. They must never know.

It would be so much easier if I could hate you. Instead, I send you my sympathy. What you are living through must be a far worse hell than anything I will ever experience. At least I have absolutely no doubt about my sex. I am female and thankful that there is no question about that in my mind. Even though I hate the whole concept of the divorce, I see now that it may have saved me from an unendurable situation. You have my sympathy but very little of my love. The man I loved doesn't exist anymore. What is left is some pathetic creature without a true identity.

Sadly,
Adrianne

May 13, 1972

Dear Andrew,

Today I almost proved to myself that I was beyond hope. I did a load of washing and put it in the dryer. Sometime later, the dryer clicked off. I came out to put in another load of clothes. When I opened the dryer and checked the clothes, they were still wet. I figured that I probably forgot to turn it on. So I turned it back on and did some other important things like stare at the ceiling. Time really flies when you are staring at your favorite crack in the ceiling. This time I distinctly remembered hearing the dryer in operation. Therefore, when I opened it and discovered all the clothes were still wet, I was confused. All I need is a repair bill. I took the bottom off of the dryer, and the belt was on. I turned the dryer on and the inside went around. The problem seemed to be a lack of hot air. With me around, it is hard to imagine not having enough hot air. I was standing there getting ready to call the repair man when I noticed that the lever marked heat had not been pushed. Somehow I had hit the air cycle instead of the heat cycle. Imagine, it only took me three hours to figure that out.

You may be confused and sick, but you were one good repairman. I shall miss many of your talents. Even though I realize a great part of your problem, I still can't reconcile myself to being alone. Without you, I feel incomplete. I keep thinking that with medical help this could have been worked out. Family life is too important to be destroyed. I feel like the clothes in the dryer. My thoughts go round and round but they don't come out dry.

Wistfully,
Adrianne

May 15, 1972

Dear Andrew,

A teacher from your school building was in the grocery store this evening. I had not seen Mary Kensington for a very long time. We talked for almost an hour. It seems that your faculty was as shocked and concerned as I was. It is hard for me to believe that you put your new wedding date on the school calendar for your teachers to see. Mary said the teachers seemed to feel that it was in very bad taste.

Mary said that she and Barbara Morris let you know they disapproved of what you were doing to me and to the children. They paid a pretty high price. I can't believe that you would embarrass and reprimand them at an open teacher's meeting. That is not like you at all. I am afraid you are moving too fast with your faculty. You may believe that what you are doing is right, but there is no way you are going to rush other people into accepting your new way of life. It doesn't work that way. It may be the twentieth century, but elementary-school principals don't divorce their wives and give up their families without criticism.

Oh, Andrew, if your faculty knew all the facts, they would ride you out of school on a rail. No, I didn't mention your strange desires. Publicity of that nature would only hurt Leslie and Scott. They have been through enough. Your secret is safe with me unless you do something unnatural.

Mary said that she had been to a party and met your new wife. Mary was not impressed. I can't believe that you got so drunk you lost your shoe in a hedge. That doesn't sound like you at all. You have gone over the deep end. That must be some married happiness if you have to drink yourself into a blind stupor to survive. Strange that suddenly you get drunk when in all our years of marriage I never saw you drink more than you could handle. You never made a fool of yourself when we went to parties. I still fear that something has happened to you to make you change so completely. If this is the manner in which you conduct yourself in public. I am glad that I never see you.

Miserably,
Adrianne

May 19, 1972

Dear Andrew,

"Count your blessings" is an old saying. That's what I am trying to do this evening. I am trying to think of all the good things about divorce. I could go on a television talk show and advocate divorce as a fantastic way to shed extra pounds. It does wonders for the figure. For some reason, I don't have any appetite. I find myself tossing and turning from 3:00 A.M. until the alarm goes off. The results are that I am back in my best clothes looking fantastic if you don't mind the deep circles around my eyes and the look of sadness that won't go away. If I could bottle the feeling of anxiety and depression and sell it for a diet drug, I'd made a fortune.

Losing twenty-five pounds is wonderful, but I think divorce is too high a price to pay for a trim figure. Men are beginning to whistle but I couldn't care less. The last thing I need is to be involved with someone else. Instead, I'll become a nun. I wonder if Protestant school teachers ever do become nuns. Devoting myself to a worthy cause might get me back into the stream of life.

There I go again, digressing from my initial purpose. I am trying to count my blessings since the divorce. Making the bed! That's a big one. I suddenly realized one morning that it didn't really matter if I made my bed or not. After all the years of married life and religiously making the bed, I discovered that the world does not end or explode if the bed is left unmade. The kids have been trying to tell me this for years. So for a whole week, I have not made my bed. It is a small pleasure, but when you are divorced you can't handle big pleasures. I can't think of any other blessings that have developed because of the divorce. I only know that there is a gigantic emptiness without you. I don't miss what you are, but I desperately miss what you were to me.

Wearily,
Adrianne

May 20, 1972

Dear Andrew,

Leslie and I have been trying to keep up with some of the yard work but it is beyond our strength and endurance. We did manage to get the riding mower started. Leslie had driven it more than I had so she decided that she would take the first section of the yard. She zeroed in on one of the small lilac bushes and cut it off at the base. Leslie felt terrible about it and so did I for awhile.

When we moved to Maryland Trail as a family, we had worked awfully hard to bring over some of the bushes and small trees that had been family gifts on Palmer Court. That was the white lilac bush that had been a Mother's Day gift to me from the children. I guess, now that I think about it, I am glad that Leslie cut it down. I don't want your second wife enjoying the lilacs from my lilac bush.

If I didn't believe in saving our plant life, I know I would be tempted to chop down all the trees and bushes we planted here. There is no way that I can move them back to Palmer Court. I do hate to think about another woman enjoying the things that represented us as a family. I hope Peg won't be able to enjoy them. I want them to remind both of you of what you have destroyed. I won't cut them down but I hope they will always have a way of reminding you of me. If Peg steps out next spring to smell the flowers from my plants, I hope a gigantic bee stings her on the end of her nose.

Bitterly,
Adrianne

May 21, 1972

Dear Andrew,

Your son may be wearing long hair but I am convinced he's not the pervert in the family. It is a strange feeling to be riding with your only son and deciding to get the map out of the glove compartment of his car to check something and to see a package of contraceptives fall out. Diplomacy is not one of my strong points. I didn't feel that I could just ignore them as they bounced off my foot. Five years of college did not offer any poetry quotes from great authors that seemed appropriate at that particular moment.

So being the modern divorced and liberated woman, I picked them up and put them back into the glove compartment. Then I told him I wasn't going to ask questions or give him a long lecture. I wasn't even going to tell him that I was disappointed because he was no longer a virgin son. I only mentioned that they were not always effective and that for every unwed mother there was an unwed father. If he got into that situation, it woud be his problem.

Scott assured me that he was aware of all that I had said. Then he added that most of the girls he dated were on the pill anyway. I can't believe I actually sat there and had that conversation with my son. I guess I am guilty of the double standard because while I could react calmly to contraceptives for my son, I wonder how I would react if it had been a different type and in my daughter's car? God, let's hope I don't have to face that issue for a long time.

Sometimes I think my children are older than I am. I seem to have led a very naive life until recently. I don't like finding out so many things so rapidly. I am not handling any of them well. I spend too much time feeling numb. I suppose I should have created a big hairy scene and made like the wounded mother but I couldn't. I guess I was secretly relieved to know my son preferred females.

Tiredly,
Adrianne

P.S. Today I started sorting tools in the garage. Thank God I looked before I asked Scott to help me. I found your box of personal pornography and sick toys. I burned the contents. Where could an elementary-school principal buy that stuff? I feel sick inside when I think of what you have become. I feel worse when I think this is how you may have been without my knowing. Where does this end?

May 31, 1972
Dear Andrew,

The pounding on my door and Danny yelling: "Adrianne! Adrianne!" woke me out of a sound sleep. All I could think of was: "Oh, My God, it's *The Graduate,* and at my age." Danny had let himself in to wait for Scott.

Danny loves the fireplace so he decided to build a fire and enjoy himself. After he got the fire started, the smoke started pouring into the living room, and he didn't know what to do, so he came up and pounded on my bedroom door. I am not at my best at one in the morning but I try.

Danny had forgotten to open the damper before he started the fire. I managed to open it without setting myself on fire. Then we opened a few windows and soon things were back to normal. Since I was awake by then, Danny and I watched the fire and talked. I like Danny. I am glad he is Scott's best friend. He has a good head on his shoulders. It will seem strange when he goes into the service soon. He won't be able to drop in at all hours of the day and night. I guess Danny is the nearest thing to the kids having an older brother. It was almost as hard to tell him about the divorce as it was to tell our own kids. His parents had been divorced for so long, he had really looked up to us as ideal parents. He can't decide whether he will speak to you or not. I think he should because he relied on you. He will need someone to talk to about the service and I think you could help him.

Scott finally came home and the three of us had a coke, and then I came upstairs. Scott and Danny will probably talk until morning. It might be nice to be young again. I envy them the honesty of their generation. They are more open, and I think this is good. If you and I had been more open in our relationship we might have worked things out. Now I'll never know.

Love,
Adrianne

June 1, 1972

Dear Andrew,

On my desk at school this morning there was a large flowerpot full of blooming plants. It looked like something you put on graves for Memorial Day. It startled me for a minute because I thought it might be a joke. Then I thought it might be from you. There was a card, and it was from my first period sophomore English class. They're a great bunch of young people. As students they were aware of how the divorce had hurt me. They have gone out of their way to be helpful and thoughtful. Some students are so considerate. They are always ready to help anyone who needs it. This is the kind of group that makes the long hours of grading papers more than worthwhile.

I am glad that I came in early because when I read the card that said "To our favorite teacher. Have a happy summer. First Period English Class," I nearly broke down. It seems like just when you think that no one in the world cares, something good happens.

I don't know how they got the plant in so early but it was a very touching way to start the last day of school before summer vacation. I will miss this group of students. I don't feel that I have been the best English teacher that I could have been because of the divorce, but I tried. Somehow this plant makes me think they understand. In the future they may need to brush up on their nouns and verbs but somewhere along the line they have learned about compassion, caring, and understanding. Those things are what really count.

Love,
Adrianne

June 6, 1972

Dear Andrew,

Three summers ago was the last time that I was in the house on Palmer Court. Everything had been washed, painted, or waxed. I remember how clean and fresh everything looked. Today I drove over to see what would have to be done before the children and I could move back in. I could not believe what was in store for me.

As I drove up I noticed that the cement wall by the steps had been broken. The screen at the front door was merely a gigantic hole. Once inside I could not believe my eyes. The floor which had once been a highly polished hardwood floor had not been touched for three years. The drapes were dirty and torn. The walls were dirty and marked with crayons. Light fixtures were broken and left hanging. This was an esoteric experience compared to my tour of the bathroom.

These people must have eaten asbestos and fungus. Both toilet bowls were filled with black sticky, fuzzy growing stuff. I hastily closed the lids for fear the stuff would spread or attack. When I tried to wash my hands at the kitchen sink, my feet got wet. When I opened the cabinet below the sink, I discovered the pipes were all broken and the drain was flooding the bottom of the cabinet, the floor, and my shoes.

I turned off the water and walked slowly back into the living room. I remember standing there in the middle of the empty room with tears welling out of my eyes. I could hear you telling me before the divorce that if the children and I moved back to Palmer Court, it would be easy to put the house in order. I remember you said that a little cleaning would have it looking like we had never left. A white tornado would not be able to put this house back in order. It might have become hysterical standing there realizing what a nightmare the place had become but about that time I felt something biting my legs. When I looked down I saw that my legs were covered with fleas. The renters had left a parting gift for me. The whole house was alive with fleas. Instead of standing there crying, I left in a hurry. Now I am trying to decide what must be done first: plumbing, cleaning, electric fixtures, etc. Where do I begin? Oh, if there were only some way to box up those fleas and mail them to you. That would be how I would begin to get ready to move. As it is, there are no words to thank you for this experience.

Disgustedly,
Adrianne

41

Dear Andrew,

Our firstborn child gave the valedictorian's speech at the Eastside High School commencement tonight. As I sat there, I suddenly felt very, very old and very, very tired. A lot of living and loving goes into producing a son like that. I'm proud of him. Scott looked tall and distinguished as he spoke to the audience. I felt so many emotions as I sat there and watched and listened. In my mind's eye, I could see you holding Scott in your arms when we brought him home from the hospital. You were so proud of our new son. I wonder if you were in the audience this evening. I didn't want to look because I was afraid you might have brought your whole new family, and I was not up to that.

Tonight was our moment. It was a time when you and I should have been able to look at each other and smile. Together we could have said that it had all been worthwhile. Instead we were separated by different worlds. I hope that time will prove that the best of both of us will exist within our son and daughter.

It's so very quiet tonight that I hear the memories of nineteen years ringing in my thoughts. Once again I am caught up in the past. Tonight I don't mind. It is good to remember the happy times. I hope that tonight you will remember too.

Love,
Adrianne

P.S. You sent me a dozen roses when Scott was born. I suppose if you had it to do over again you would send me a cactus.

June 10, 1972

Dear Andrew,

The children and I just came back from Palmer Court. The exterminators got rid of the fleas for the small sum of thirty-five dollars. We took the cleaning materials over and started to work. They were going to wash the walls in the living room while I tackled the toilets.

I had rubber gloves and steel wool. It took three hours of scraping to clean two toilet bowls. During the three hours I cried, swore, and gave up. Mentally I am in no condition to do what has to be done before we can move back. The children tried but we can't face what needs to be done.

Hard work is supposed to be great for curing depression but I guess I am not ready to be cured. I should have given you custody of the children, and then I could have disappeared. But then, as I recall, you didn't want the responsibility of the children. You wanted to be free to start a new life. You wanted me to be free to do my own thing. Somehow scraping a mess of black crud out of a filthy toilet bowl is not conducive to visions of a new life. All I could think of was that I'd probably get VD.

This is the kind of day that I find myself hoping you develop a large and painful boil on the end of your you know what.

Love,
Adrianne

P.S. I am going to take the easy way out. I called a professional cleaning company. They are going to put the house in order for one hundred and fifty dollars. I am only sorry you don't have to pay for it.

June 12, 1972

Dear Andrew,

For three weeks one of Scott's loving friends has been staying with us. Lowell dropped out of school and had no place to go. It gave me a funny feeling to know he was in the house when I left to go shopping, but I could not bring myself to throw him out. Lowell seemed in his own personal world of misery. If giving him a place to stay and a little food would help him get his head together, I couldn't throw him out. Scott and I have said little but there has been a lot of tension. Three weeks with a stranger in the house is difficult.

43

Tonight I realized that Lowell wasn't in the house. I asked Scott what time Lowell would be back. Scott informed me that Lowell was a no-good deadbeat and that he would not have him hanging around the house any longer. Lowell accepted no responsibility toward taking care of himself. He figured that someone would look after him. For a time it worked. Then Scott realized what was happening. I do feel a little sorry for Lowell. It is a lonely world and everybody needs to believe that there is at least one person who cares. Caring is a two-way situation and Scott discovered that he was more concerned about Lowell's well-being than Lowell was.

Lowell will manage somehow. The takers in this world always seem to keep taking. It seems that Lowell took our portable tape recorder and my jar of change with him when he left. There could be other things missing, but I don't want to take inventory. Patience and keeping my cool may have allowed Scott to learn an important lesson in growing up. I hope he realizes that individuals have to work and do their share to be respected and appreciated. If Scott learns this, it was worth the price of the tape recorder and the change. Growing up is painful. It is particularly painful for me. I am almost forty, and suddenly I have a lot of growing up to do.

Love,
Adrianne

June 26, 1972

Dear Andrew,

On this day the children and I came back to Palmer Court. Somehow before the divorce when we talked to each other, it seemed like a good idea for you to help the children and me move our belongings. Today, with you married to another woman, it was a nightmare. It would have been worth any price to have an impersonal mover carry our belongings from one house to another.

Somehow, when your father drove up with the trucks and his hired hands, it brought back so many memories of things we had all done together that I did not think I could face the agony of moving. Fortunately for me, you were in rare form. Never before have I seen you act like a one hundred percent super-rare bastard. I did not have to be concerned in any way that you would be a good sport about an awkward situation.

You kept your word. You moved us and in no way did you spare me a single scratch, blemish, or curse. Your hatred was magnificent and unbearable. I think you might have spared the feelings of the children and your father. They were very uncomfortable.

Oh, I was delighted that you noticed that the house on Maryland Trail is filthy. After I saw the rental property, I gave up any pretense of cleaning on Maryland Trail. I figured my parting gift to you would be as much dirt and filth as I could possibly accumulate before I left. When you asked if I planned on coming back to clean up the place, I hope you noticed that I did smile when I said no.

There is some small satisfaction in knowing that you and your new family will have to clean up my dirt. Andrew, I know you so well. There is no way that you would spend money to hire someone to clean up the house. I will enjoy knowing that your new and devoted wife will be able to work at your side while you call me terrible names. I hope that the dog shit will have time to dry where it is mashed into the deep pile carpet. I'm just sorry I couldn't transplant some of the growth from the Palmer Court toilets to the three toilets on Maryland Trail. That would have been the perfect touch. I hope you will think of me as you find all the delicate little reminders that I have left.

Love,
Adrianne

P.S. I still think of you as you were, not as you have become. In that respect I miss you deeply.

45

Dear Andrew,

You proved a point that I did not believe. I had been told that if it was not in writing, it had no meaning. I did not believe this. I believed that if you made a verbal agreement it was binding. Andrew, you are no longer a man of your word. Today you came after the second car. I know it was registered in your name but I thought we had an understanding that since Scott was going to college, Lesile would take over the Mercury so that she would have transportation to school.

Well, Andrew, you aren't as clever as you thought. You may have taken the car but the snow tires are in the basement. You will never see them again. I can be bitter too. It may be July, but I hope we have an early snow so that you get stuck.

Talking to you on the phone is a bad trip. Since you did not leave a note saying you had taken the car, you are lucky that I called you before I called the police. I thought it had been stolen. In a sense it had been. You stole the car from your daughter so the new broad would have transportation. That's really pretty crummy. It irritates me to think that you no longer live up to your word. I thought you were one of the few people in the world who was honorable about a verbal agreement. That has to be the funniest thing I have written yet. You have lied to me since the beginning of this whole mess, and I am still dumb enough to think your word is a binding agreement. I truly am falling apart. I'm glad you think that your daughter should take the bus. Leslie is always delighted that you care for her in such a fatherly manner. You bastard, I hope the car turns on you and runs over you.

Hatefully,
Adrianne

P.S.   We will not suffer over the loss of the Mercury. It was a gas hog. Mother bought a new Vega and gave Leslie the Nova.

Happy birthday to our daughter,

Andrew, our daughter is seventeen today. It is difficult to believe that she is so grown up. Scott, Mark, and I had a small dinner and a birthday cake for her. I thought you might have called to say something special to her. You were so proud of her when she was born. You made me believe that she was the most wonderful baby girl in the world. Where are you today when Leslie needs to know that she is still the most wonderful girl in the world?

You did remember to send a package. If you did not plan on getting her something she wanted, why did you ask what she wanted? Leslie likes to sew, and she wanted double knit material because that is what is popular now. I won't forget the look of disappointment on her face when she opened the package and saw the blue and white material that had all the softness of starched canvas. The tent company must have been having a sale.

It did not make it any easier to open the card and find out that Peg had picked it out. We didn't need to be told. It was in such poor taste that it was obvious that Peg had picked it out. Whether you realize it or not, that just blew the brownie points for your new wife. Leslie will never meet her now, she is afraid the poor taste is contagious. Look what it has done for you!

Sadly,
Adrianne

Dear Andrew,

A wife loses many things in the process of divorce but I have been very slow in realizing that I don't have any friends. For some reason the people I know and socialized with were the people directly related to your school and your work. No wonder my phone never rings. People choose up sides during a divorce. The ones connected with you and your school will naturally select your side. As vindictive as you have become, they would be foolish to do otherwise.

For a long time I kept expecting the phone to ring. I thought someone would feel they would like to have lunch with me. I believed a voice would say: "Why don't you have lunch with me, Adrianne?" or "Let's take in a movie." It won't happen because the people I knew would feel like they were being disloyal to you. With your attitude they can't afford to be seen with me. The people I know at my school don't realize how alone I am. I guess I am going to have to find a whole new set of friends. That may not be easy when you are divorced and thirty-nine. Most people have their circles of friends. They aren't interested in enlarging it, especially to include a woman alone.

One of these days I will stop staring into space and pick up the phone and call someone. It looks like I will have to make the first move. I guess the first one is the hardest. It must be because I don't even know whom to call. I would call you but I doubt if your wife would let you go to the show with me. Maybe if I offered to pay your way, we could work it out.

Love,
Adrianne

July 26, 1972

Dear Andrew,

Walking into the living room, I tripped over one of Leslie's shoes. Then I looked around and there were at least four pairs of shoes that belonged to her. Shoes were all over the living room. I started to cry. It has been a long time since Scott told her she could keep her shoes in the living room since you wouldn't be around to holler at her for being careless. Leslie has never forgotten that, and I never say: "Put your shoes away." It's her way of coping with losing you, and I respect it.

Still, today it made me cry. I wanted you to be here to say: "Leslie Ann, put those shoes away." It's only a small wish, but it's my way of wanting family living to be back to normal. When will I learn that to you family living is not normal? After I cried, I put her shoes away and sat very still for a long time. Sometimes I don't believe I even think. I simply sit and do nothing. Turning everything off is my way of coping. It is not very effective.

Love,
Adrianne

August, 2, 1972

Dear Andrew,

Forty-seven dollars and fifty cents would purchase a small revolver at Air-Mart. I did not realize that it could be so easy to walk in and buy a gun. For quite awhile I have very seriously considered the possibility of shooting myself. I know that taking a life, even one's own, is wrong, yet I can't think of any reason for living.

It would be so easy to buy the gun and come home and use it. Then I would not have to think about anything anymore. Thinking is what is destroying me. I keep wanting to understand why this had to happen to me. Is it my fault that you changed? Or did you change? Have you always been this way? If you were always strange, why didn't I recognize what was happening? Why am I on the earth? What is the point of living? The questions go on and on until they haunt me. I can't find any answers, and I can't really talk to anyone.

People know I am depressed, and they really try to be helpful but there is no way I can explain the personal hell that I am trapped within. All my life I have behaved in a fairly logical manner. I believe in cause and effect, in action and reaction. Now there is nothing that I can understand. I have always believed that there is a reason why everything happens. I can't find any reason to explain my life.

49

Worst of all is not being able to laugh. All through my life when things went wrong I could see humor in the situation. I could break the tension by smiling or laughing. This ability is gone. Nothing is funny. The pain of the divorce is over but the raw emptiness keeps eating away at my very being. I don't have any identity to call my own. I am so tired of trying to find myself that I want to give up.

This is not fair to the children or to my mother but does life have to be fair to anyone? Today I would have bought the gun but I honestly believed that if I would try to shoot myself, I'd miss and make things worse. I picture my suicide in a step-by-step fashion, and I know that at this point I could pull the trigger and end this mistake that is my life. I suppose I could do it, and yet, I am waiting. I don't know why I am waiting but I am. Buying a gun is not the answer at this point. Oh, Andrew, I wonder if you are as unhappy as I am.

Miserably,
Adrianne

August 7, 1972
Dear Andrew,

It was not my favorite day. It was not easy for Scott to drive over to Maryland Trail to his former home. Joining you and your new family in our former dining room was difficult for my son. I am not sure but what it was a high price for him to pay for a dinner. I hope you tried to understand some of his feelings. Only a short time earlier that house had been his home. Fortunately, Scott has my bitter sense of humor. The fact that your living room was now decorated in bright green and vivid orange helped. The cheap velvet paintings on the wall enabled him to survive. There is nothing more suggestive of a cheap woman than her cheap taste in home decorating. Scott described your new furnishings as a Nu-Mart Furniture nightmare. For a

50

young man interested in antiques, that was the worst insult he could give your furniture. I guess the orange ball fringe around the drapes, the pillows, the ends of the chairs, and the table coverings really cracked him up. Somehow you and Peg had destroyed the natural beauty of the house to the point where he could survive by laughing instead of crying. He thought he would miss the fireplace the most, but when he saw that she had glued orange ball fringe on the glass front enclosure he managed to hang on.

Scott was very polite about the whole situation. He said that when he first sat down at the table, he was tempted to ask for a menu, but he controlled himself. He wanted me to laugh so that I would not be upset by his going over there. He mentioned that Peg served a fine meal. She was very efficient at serving and removing dishes. Peg was right in there to keep those water glasses and coffee cups filled.

This was the first time that Scott had talked to your stepchildren at close range. He described them in his best dry manner. He insists that Marie looks like Hardy and that Judy looks like Laurel. He had the strange feeling that before the meal was over they would do a comedy routine. Instead they sat there in an uncomfortable silence. There were a lot of uncomfortable silences during the evening.

I wonder what you think you have proved? Scott has met Peg. He has met the stepchildren. He has eaten a meal in your house. You may think it was the beginning of a loving family group, but you have a way of underestimating our son. Scott went but I know that he insulted you and your waitress wife at every opportunity. You may not have realized it, but he did. He is like a time bomb waiting to go off. I feel sorry for you because you are not bright enough to see what is happening. His use of irony would not register with you immediately. It would be after Scott left that you would ponder over his words and then get angry knowing that he had intended to insult you and your precious waitress. Being the dutiful son has become a game with Scott.

It is a destructive game that he will play to win at your expense. I almost feel sorry for you, but not quite.

Love,
Adrianne

August 9, 1972

Dear Andrew,

Emptiness surrounds me and I think I may buy the gun after all. There really isn't any point in trying to hold on. Without you I have no identity. This whole situation is completely insane. This is alien to any form of life that I am able to comprehend. There should be some switch that could be flipped off to end a useless life.

I never will forget one evening shortly after you began talking about a divorce. I was crying and trying to keep my sanity by making funny comments that were not funny. I was so tired and so confused. I remember saying that I couldn't decide if it would be better to shoot you or myself. It was just one of those ridiculous things you say and forget immediately.

The funny part was that you thought I was capable of shooting you. You took the rifle, the shells, and a chair to prop against the inside of the bedroom door. Somehow it seems ludicrous to think of a man that I loved for so many years propping a chair under the doorknob so that I would not be able to come in and destroy you during your sleep. I wonder if you slept any that night? I can see all six foot, two hundred pounds of you cowering under the covers. Shooting you could have been a better solution. I'll never really know.

Noise, mess, and cowardliness keep me from using a gun on either of us. Maybe people do die of broken hearts. If so, that may be the solution. Mine is not only broken but smashed and discarded. Tomorrow has to be better.

Wearily,
Adrianne

Dear Andrew,

My mood is worse so I decided to check back with the doctor. In this day of miracle drugs there is certainly one that will wipe out the pain of a divorce. Sitting in the doctor's office, I couldn't help but remember the hours we have spent there with the children. That office used to be our home away from home. There are a great many memories of our family life in that waiting room.

I never will forget the time that you had the kidney infection that would not end. You had to keep going back and each time you had to take in a urine specimen. I remember going with you to the doctor's office. You gave the nurse the specimen bottle. A little later we heard her laughing and laughing. Instead of a regular specimen, you had given her a bottle of water with two baby guppies swimming frantically. She had set the bottle by the microscope and when she went to pick up a slide she saw something move in the bottle. She couldn't believe it at first, and then she could not stop laughing. Those are the crazy things that I miss now that we are no longer together.

Dr. Smith was very kind today but not too encouraging. He knows I have been deeply hurt and time alone will be the answer. He can give me tranquilizers to calm me down and to help me sleep but he can't give me a pill to make me happy. That will come from me or it won't happen. What I am going through is typical and normal in terms of a divorce but being a statistic doesn't make me feel any better. I feel very much alone. It is hard to believe that this happens all the time and that people do survive. I will try to hang on but I must admit that death seems preferable to being so alone and so unhappy. Please let me smile again soon.

Love,
Adrianne

Dear Andrew,

"Are you Andrew's wife?" seems to be the hardest question in the world for me to answer. For some reason, it is the one I am most frequently asked. It seems to happen wherever I go. Today I was putting a dress on lay-a-way at Sears and as soon as I gave my name the clerk had to ask if I was your wife. When I told her that I was your former wife, she still had to go into a five-minute routine on the fact that she had been one of your former students. People don't understand that there is a wide difference between being a former wife and a former student. You were the best teacher the clerk had ever had. You were so nice to her when she needed someone to talk to. Well, dammit, if you are so nice, where are you when I need someone to talk to?

I am glad you were a good teacher. I am glad that your former students think so highly of you but I hate to be asked if I'm your wife. I used to take such pride in being Andrew's wife. Now it's a nightmare situation. Maybe I should take out a billboard advertisement that says: "Attention World! Adrianne Helman is no longer the current wife of Andrew H. Helman. She has been replaced by a waitress." I don't know why I am so sensitive. I guess in time I will get used to this situation. Supposedly, in time, people get used to anything. Well, time, do your work. I'm not used to this situation, and I don't think I ever will be. I wonder how long it takes to stop feeling like your wife? Even with all that has happened, I feel married to you. I guess I just don't know how to feel like a person who is unmarried.

Love,
Adrianne

Dear Andrew,

Your son, the thundercloud, just told me in no uncertain terms that he had quit his job at the public library. Or in his words, "They can take that page's job and shove it!" I'm not used to hearing him talk or act in that manner. Scott used to be so quiet and reserved. Now he is a bundle of animosities. He is hair-triggered in his temper and spoiling for a fight. Visiting with you does not improve his dispostion.

I tried to be diplomatic and get him to soothe over the problem at the library, since he might need a job reference someday, but he was not buying anything rational at this time. He is looking for ways to lash out at the world because he can't lash out at us. Scott can't poke you in the nose so he is poking everything else. Divorce has a way of bringing out the worst and the best of us as individuals.

The young rebel is a hero in his own eyes and in the eyes of his friends, and maybe that is all that matters right now. The job would have only lasted for a few more days because he will soon be leaving for Fenton College. Scott did have a point in his favor. If all that he was doing was moving newspapers and magazines in the library, it looks like he could have worn his cut-offs. Since he was in the attic he would not have destroyed any public image. At least he let off steam. It may have been good for him. In this world you either get ulcers or you give them. It seems like he has decided to become one of the givers. With a little luck, he may even give you one.

Love,
Adrianne

Dear Andrew,

Middletown has very little to offer in the way of excitement for a divorced woman of my age. I find myself at a loss for diversion. Sometimes I have to get out of the house but there are few choices of where I may go. Yes, I am sure I could guess where you might suggest. The climate is a little too warm but otherwise I doubt if hell is much different than the life I have now.

Tonight I went out to Air-Mart to see if they were having any special sales. They weren't. It is surprising the number of people that are found in a discount store in the evening. They don't seem to be buying but simply moving around. I wonder how many of them are as lonely as I am? I can understand the number of families moving around. It is a kind of indoor entertainment, and there are always some things on sale that the members of a young family may use. I find myself amazed at the number of people alone that seem to be wandering around. They can't all be shoplifters. I am tempted to take a survey to see how many of them are either widowed or divorced. Air-Mart might be missing a million-dollar business by not offering a dating service.

Can't you imagine a green light special for five minutes that offers a choice of dates with any one of twenty-five men between the ages of thirty and thirty-five? For only $19.98 you get four hours of fun that includes two hamburgers, two Cokes, and three games at the bowling alley with one of the men. Rental for the bowling shoes would be extra. Then a half an hour later there would be a green light special offering one evening of entertainment and excitement with the bargain of the night. That would be your choice of ten men from ages 65 to 80 all of whom would be five feet one or less in height. This date would only cost you $10.98 but you would have to provide your own transportation from the nursing home. Now I am being terrible, but it has been a rotten evening.

I find myself walking up and down the aisles wanting to scream to anyone: "Please talk to me." This loneliness is unendurable and yet I keep hanging on. There must be an answer soon. There has to be.

Love,
Adrianne

August 30, 1972

Dear Andrew,

Will you remember that today is my birthday? I notice you did not remember to send a card or flowers. Perhaps they will come later. After all a fortieth birthday should be special. The children outdid themselves. I could not believe it when I opened the package. There was a black box from Larry Faunt's Jewelry Store. Inside was a lovely diamond on a silver chain. I was deeply touched. It had been Scott's idea. He and Leslie had been saving for a very long time to purchase it.

I doubt if you will understand the significance of it, but I do. The children remembered a birthday a long time ago when all I got was a plastic funnel and a record book. The neighbor across the street a few days earlier had received a diamond pendant from her husband. Our finances at that time were in very bad shape. You joked and said that in time you would buy me a diamond big enough to fit in the plastic funnel. All I had to do was to stick with you and someday I would have my diamond. Well, I tried to stick with you but I never got the diamond. Finally, I even lost you. For some reason, it was important to Scott and Leslie that the promise of a diamond pendant be kept.

The diamond would never fill the plastic funnel but the love of those children filled my heart. They are two very special young people. You should be proud of them. Without them, I would have cut my wrists a long time ago. Because of them, I will hang on. This will even out. I will survive. Life begins at forty. Today I am forty. I am ready for my life to begin. Anything at this point could only be an improvement.

Love,
Adrianne

September 1, 1972

Dear Andrew,

Scott came home from having dinner with you and with Peg. I could tell that he was upset more than usual. He was not amused at Peg telling him that she wanted to be a mother. Scott is the only Helman to represent your family by name and heritage, and that's the way it should remain. I promised him that there would not be another Helman brought into this world by Peg. I always keep my promises.

For last Christmas, mother gave me a strange gift. She had been to an auction for a doctor who had been a world traveler. She bought several unusual items to wrap up for jokes. I remember when I picked up one of the Christmas packages, I shuddered. Inside the package was a strange and ugly doll. I closed the box immediately because I knew that the doll was evil. When I gained control and looked at it carefully I knew that this was a powerful voodoo doll or image of evil. It was made out of what looked like coconut fibers. The craftsmanship was crude but careful. The fingernails and toenails were made of bits of pine cones. The doll wore a copper bracelet and around its neck was a metal chain with a small piece of unusual rock. It had a strange nose, a braided tail, and grass-like skirt. I don't believe in witchcraft, voodoo, or any of the other superstitions, yet I knew that this came to me for a reason.

I was icy cold inside, and I could hardly bring myself to touch the doll. I finally made some joke about it and put it back in the box. I went on opening the packages but there was a chill feeling of fear inside me. There was a reason why that doll was to be in my possession, and it frightened me. After Christmas I wrapped the doll carefully in a black silk handkerchief and tissue paper. Then I put it away knowing there would be a time when I would need it.

You always joked about my grandmother having been a witch. I joked with you. My grandmother was a seventh daughter, and she knew many things. I never wanted her powers and yet I have always known that I had them. Tonight they must be called into action. I unwrapped the doll. The evil was overpowering. What I did tonight had to be done for my son and for my daughter. There is a limit to what I will take from you and from your new wife. It would have been easy to place the pins in the heart of the doll but death is not the answer. When I resort to evil, I must be ready for the consequences. There is always an action and a reaction. Therefore, I had to be careful in what I decided to do. This act will cost me two years of personal pain and sadness but the pins with the red heads must be placed in the doll. The doll was given the name of Peg Helman, the words of vengeance were stated, and then the pins with the red heads were placed in the lower part of the doll's body. It is done and there is no way I can change what will happen. There will be pain, and Peg Helman will never be the mother of your child. The heritage of my children is safe. I left the pins in place, and I rewrapped the doll in the black silk handkerchief and put it carefully away. Only time will tell.

Divorce is destroying me, and I think some days that I am quite mad. I can lie for hours staring at a crack in the ceiling. I am afraid to take a bath without someone in the house. I spend hours wanting to die. My nerves are shot, and the doctor says I am in a deep depression. These things are facts. Certainly, the action with the doll is a form of complete mental breakdown. It should be. Instead it is the most rational step I have taken since the divorce. It shows that I am still alive enough to fight for my children. There is some hope for me.

Love,
Adrianne

September 5, 1972

Dear Andrew,

So many times when I write to you it is because I am crying. This time I can't help but laugh. Your latest phone call was a priceless moment in history. I can't believe that you would actually call me to tell me that I would have to do something about Leslie harassing your new wife and stepdaughter. For a minute I was really concerned because I could imagine all kinds of terrible things that might have happened. Emotionally I was prepared for the worst.

When you told me that Leslie had driven by the house on Maryland Trail with a friend and flipped Peg and Marie the bird, I had to laugh. It is the first time I have laughed in a long time. Somehow the picture of Leslie being driven slowly past her former home holding her middle finger up in the air at Peg and Marie cracks me up. There is hope for Leslie yet. How fortunate that the one time Leslie drove by Peg and Marie happened to be where they would see her make this obscene gesture.

It was even funnier to think that a principal would go into such a tirade over such a small impulsive act. What kind of an adult is your new wife that she can't accept such a gesture in the spirit it was given? Leslie has no love for her. Peg destroyed Leslie's way of life. Marie is sleeping in Leslie's former bedroom and receiving the attention that Leslie used to receive from you. I think that you are damn lucky that she flipped her middle finger and not a hand grenade. I can't help but think a mature woman would have ignored the gesture and not even mentioned it to you.

You're so busy being upset about your waitress that you are forgetting about your own daughter. I know the waitress may get angry and spill hot soup on you, but stop and think for a minute. Leslie must be pretty unhappy if she is reacting like this. Aren't you at all concerned about her?

There is no way that I will punish Leslie for the gesture. You have punished her enough for a lifetime. If your new wife is upset, I am sure that you will comfort her. If Peg will feel better, you have my permission to drive by here and let her flip the bird at me. As for your having Leslie arrested if she does this again, I don't think that flipping the bird at one person is against the law. I am afraid you would be very unhappy to know that Scott, Leslie, and I laughed a very long time over this incident. We are thinking about getting a caravan of friends together to drive by and one by one slow down and flip the bird at Peg. If I call and arrange a time, could you have her standing at the front window to get the full effect?

If you are talking about arrests, I do want to make one comment. I meant it when I told you over the phone that if you ever call Leslie and read her the riot act before you notify me, I will have your rights taken away from you. She does not have to take that kind of talk from you. You did not swear at her when we were married, and you are not going to swear at her now. What a refreshing change. This time I swore at you until you hung up. I am getting stronger after all. Well, here's my middle finger to you!

Pointedly,
Adrianne

September 7, 1972

Dear Andrew,

Scott hasn't really been home since the divorce started but today it was different. He carried his suitcases out to the car. Then he came in to kiss me good-bye and tell me he was off to conquer Fenton College. I am glad he has a chance to go away to school but in my heart I know he won't like it. With our lives in a turmoil, he would have been better off to stay at home and attend Mason State College. Scott's natural interest in antiques will keep calling him back. Since he has gotten acquainted with Jeff, I can tell that antiques are his first love. Jeff is near Scott's age and has an antique shop.

I am so glad that you talked to Scott about college.

I think he needs to listen to both of us. I won't say anything about the fraternity but I can't picture our son as a fraternity jock. Scott is too much of an individual. He simply will not be able to do the ridiculous things that are required to become a member of a group. I know you could, and that was fine for you. Scott is different. I know that I never could go the sorority route because I did not want to be like everyone else. Scott may surprise me but I bet he doesn't last a week in a fraternity house. If he becomes a big man on campus, it will be because of his individual efforts.

There were so many things I wanted to say to Scott before he left. I had a million words of wisdom but I didn't say any of them. He has heard my words of wisdom for eighteen years. Now he will have to live them or find his own. The saddest part was knowing that he had grown up and that he would never again come home. This is the first step in finding his own home, and I won't hold him back. My two men are gone. Somehow I will hang on. There has to be a reason, and I will find it.

Love,
Adrianne

September 8, 1972

Dear Andrew,

As a teacher I committed the unpardonable sin. I told Eastside High School that I didn't care if my daughter took academic English. Imagine the reaction that I received as an English teacher. The Eastside counselor thinks I am insane. He is probably right. Leslie and I discussed it. She doesn't want to take the academic English class. I told her she could take as few classes as possible as long as she graduated, kept the house clean, and had my supper ready when I got home from school. At this point she doesn't plan on going to college, and I am not going to force her.

Needless to say, the counselor was very upset with me. He felt that I should insist on her taking more classes.

I figure the last thing Leslie needs is for me to insist that she sit in classes she would hate. Her basic spoken and written language is better than most students, so I am not going to worry about it. That's not true. I will worry about it but I will not make her any more unhappy than she already is. You, Andrew, have given her enough sadness for both of us.

I still hope she will consider going to Mason State College for at least one quarter but it will have to be her decision. If she will be happier getting a job I won't object. I'm glad someone will do the housework. When I get home I am ready to collapse. The days all run together and the nights are tears and frustration. Will this mood ever pass? I miss you so much I feel like I am dying inside. Even when I know the worst about you, I still need the security of a complete family.

Helplessly,
Adrianne

September 14, 1972

Dear Andrew,
Your dreams of a fraternity son have just been flushed down the cesspool of life. Scott came in from Fenton College for the weekend. He had moved out of the fraternity house into a dorm. I was curious so he told me what had happened.

One of the fraternity members was a big jock who ran around the frat house flexing his muscles and blowing on a conch shell. His favorite outfit was a small bikini. Scott had tried to avoid him but one night the body beautiful saw Scott get ready to go out the door. Tarzan yelled: "Hey, pledge, go get me some beer." This is common practice, so Scott picked up the money and asked Tarz what kind he wanted. Tarz made the mistake of saying: "Any kind you drink, pledge." When Scott came back, Tarz went out of his tree. You see, Scott came back with a six pack of root beer. Tarz was livid when he asked why. Scott just smiled and said it was the kind that he drank. This type of humor is not appreciated by super jocks.

The jock's hostile reaction convinced Scott that he was not cut out for fraternity life. He moved his stuff into the car and spent the night in a parking lot. The next morning he moved into a dorm. I thought it was beautiful. It restored my faith in my son's natural intelligence. There is hope for us yet. He is very excited about Fenton College but he misses working with antiques. He has spent all his spare time visiting antique shops in the area. I was so glad to see him. I told him to call you but he said next time he came back he would call you. For a little while we were a family, and it was good. I missed him more than I realized.

Love,
Adrianne

September 16, 1972

Dear Andrew,
Leslie was very upset when I came home from school. I always panic a little because I am afraid that the very worst has happened. She said she had something terrible to tell me but she didn't know how to do it. I didn't know what to expect. I tried to explain that I loved her and that she could tell me anything. Then she said: "It's not about me, it's about Kathy, and I don't want you to think badly of her." I told her that I wasn't going to think badly of her friend no matter what it was that she had to tell me.

Slowly and with many tears, she told me that Kathy wasn't even sixteen, and now she was pregnant. Her boyfriend, Doug, was only sixteen. They were afraid to tell her parents. So Kathy had told Leslie this afternoon and now Leslie didn't know what to do. She wanted me to talk to Kathy. Oh, my, what words of wisdom can you possibly give to a girl who's not sixteen and is pregnant? So no matter what you can say, they are only words and the girl has to face and to live through the situation. It is strange how as a teacher you lose track of the number of girls whom you have helped in a similar situation. You begin to forget their names but somehow when you are faced with a new situation you see their faces in your mind's eye. You never know if you help, you can only try.

Leslie knew that I would try to help so she pulled herself together, washed her face, and went after Kathy. Then I had to watch them both in tears. They are such good friends that it is almost as hard on Leslie as it is on Kathy. The only thing I could do was to tell Kathy what she already knew. She would have to tell her mother. There wasn't time to waste. Then I told her what she could expect from her mother. Her mother has a quick temper. I told Kathy that her mother would probably flare up and be very angry and upset. Kathy would have to understand that any mother would be hurt and angry to find this out. Then, after her mother had some time to get used to the idea, she would be all right. Once the baby arrived, her mother would love it as much as any of the other grandchildren. The main thing that Kathy would have to do would be to give her mother a chance to accept the situation without getting angry herself.

There would be many details to work out because of their ages. They were so young they would need the court's permission to marry. Doug would have to find a job. Then, too, Kathy would have to be very sure that she wanted to keep the baby and marry Doug. Once she had made up her mind, I was sure that Kathy's mother would do anything she could to make sure Kathy was happy. Kathy's father wouldn't be a problem because he was more easygoing. He accepted life as it came without losing his temper. Kathy knew she could count on him.

They got all the tears out of their system and seemed to be calmed down. Then Kathy asked Leslie if Leslie would go with her when she told her mother. I stayed out of this decision. This was something that Kathy and Leslie had to work out. Leslie knew that Kathy needed her, so she said she would go. They decided to get it over with.

Waiting for Leslie to come back was a very long experience. I felt so sorry for all of them. Sometimes life gets so complicated that it seems impossible for everyone. It was over an hour before Leslie came back. It was a sad smile that greeted me when I opened the door. There were tears in her eyes when she said it was going to be OK. Kathy's mom had been very angry at first but she finally calmed down. When Leslie left they were starting to untangle the problems that lay ahead of them. I have great sympathy for Kathy and her family but I am selfish in being thankful it wasn't Leslie.

Love,
Adrianne

September 18, 1972

Dear Andrew,

Life does have a sense of humor. There is even irony in my teaching. I checked my schedule of nine-week Phase Elective English classes and discovered that during the first nine-week period of the second semester I will be teaching a class called Love Makes the World Go 'Round. By now I should be an expert because I can honestly say that love made my world go round and round and round. As a matter of fact I am still reeling from the impact.

It does seem a little warped that a divorced woman will be teaching young girls a class on love. It might be a good idea, but how to keep the bitterness from showing will be a problem. Girls should see the side of love with the stars taken out of it. They need to think about what it would be like to live in a story that doesn't end with the old cliche: "And they all lived happily ever after." I will have to do some work on this class. Somehow I will have to maintain a balance for the sake of the girls who take the class. It would be terrible to destroy their dreams.

We all need dreams to heal the wounds that reality leaves. The best way to handle the class will be to stick with the stories and the poems and stay away from personal experiences. I doubt if many of them will realize that I am divorced, or if they do they won't see the funny side of this teaching situation. I am not sure that I really see the funny side. Oh, love of long ago, please put my world together.

Hopefully,
Adrianne

September 23, 1972

Dear Andrew,

The books on poison at the library are of absolutely no value if you are looking for a way to kill yourself in a painless fashion. The authors of poison books only succeed in scaring the hell out of you. I decided I could not buy a gun and shoot myself because of the noise and the mess. So I decided to check on poison. I could save my tranquilizers but there is no way to judge their strength in terms of how many it would take to put me to sleep on a permanent basis.

Poison seemed to be a nice quiet way of solving my problems. I knew I could not walk into the nearest drugstore and say: "Pardon me, I am going to commit suicide, could you suggest a painless, efficient pill that would not be too expensive?" I thought the library would surely have a book that would give me the information that I needed. Poison is not an exact way to die. There are too many side effects, and some of them have a great deal of pain and misery connected with them. I couldn't take that.

As an English teacher I remember reading about death by poison. It always seemed quiet and dignified—you merely drank your coffee, tea, or wine and drifted off to the big school in the sky.

Things are pretty rotten when you can't even kill yourself.

Love,
Adrianne

September 29, 1972

Dear Andrew,

Timothy Jackson stayed after class today. He never has very much to say; he is one of the quiet ones who tries his best and never causes any trouble. I was a little puzzled when I looked up and saw him standing there by my desk. His eyes were brimming with tears and there was a small quaver in his voice when he told me that it had been a terrible weekend at his house. His father had told the family that he was fed up with all of them and that he was going to file for a divorce. For one awful moment, I thought I was going to cry. I could remember what it was like when it happened to me. Falling apart wouldn't help Timothy but it was painful to be calm.

Timothy was saying, "Oh, Mrs. Helman, I love my mother and my father. I don't want this to happen. What can I do?" How could I tell him that there wasn't anything he could do? There weren't any easy answers. Fathers have to do what they think is best, and sometimes that includes hurting the children they love. I tried to tell Timothy that sometimes adults make hasty decisions. With time, his father might change his mind. Then Timothy really cried. It seems that after Timothy was supposed to be asleep, he heard his parents talking. His father had been dating another woman and wanted to marry her. Well, I'll say one thing for Timothy's father, he was honest about the situation. It may have been painful but he was honest and open about the situation. Timothy heard his father leave. Then he heard his mother crying. He went in to comfort her but he did not know what to say.

Finally, I couldn't stand hearing any more so I just put

my arms around Timothy and said, "I don't know if this will help you or not but divorce happened to me and to my children. It hurt us deeply to lose a husband and father, but somehow the children and I managed. I can't give you any magic solution but I can tell you that some way, somehow, it works out. Divorce hurts a lot but it does work out. You are going to have to be very strong and very understanding so that you will be able to help your mother. She is going to need all the love that you can give her. You are the oldest. You are going to have to help with your brother and sisters. I can't say that you will ever understand why the divorce happens to your family but you will learn to live with the situation." Timothy and I talked for a little longer. That was the first time I have ever talked about my divorce to a student. I didn't think I would ever be able to say the words. But when I saw how sad and hurt Timothy was I had to try and help him. Maybe there is some comfort in knowing that someone else has faced a problem you have to deal with. I told him I'd be in my room if he needed to talk. I was glad it was my preparation period, I don't think I could have taught right then.

Divorce is painful and there is no way to make it easy. I hate to think what the next few weeks will be like for Timothy and for his family. I can't help but think that the divorce laws are too lenient. People should stay together and work out their problems if they have families. I still believe that divorce is a luxury that should not be tolerated. When two people make a commitment and bring children into the world, they should abide by that commitment. This is not a modern attitude but sometimes I think I am at heart a very traditional conservative. Hang on, Timothy! The pain doesn't end but it gets softer with time.

Thoughtfully,
Adrianne

P.S.   Do you ever miss me?

Dear Andrew,

With all my heart I wish you were Scott's legal guardian. I can't believe that he is real. He has absolutely no common sense at all. I received a bill from the Middletown Public Library, and Scott owes them $172.30 in library fines. He must have half of the public library checked out.

When he comes home from Fenton College this weekend he will have some tall explaining to do. I know that he had checked out books for some of his friends but this is impossible. The library has him charged with books, magazines, pamphlets, records, and artwork. When we moved from Maryland Trail, I made him take all the things he had checked out back to the library.

When Scott worked there as a page, I know that he had special privileges but I can't believe that they would let him take that much stuff out unless he took some of it back. That is the type of carelessness in him that reminds me of you.

What would you do in a situation like this? Why do I get all the problems? Teaching six English classes a day at Sushawanee High School is complicated enough without coming home to a library bill that staggers my imagination. If it is real, Scott will have to take care of it. There is no way that I will pay a bill of that size for such a foolish reason. I wonder if I will repeat that when they put me in jail for nonpayment of library fines. Scott's lack of responsibility worries me more than the actual size of the fine. He is changing because of the divorce and I don't like the change.

Tonight I will grade all my papers. I will not think of you. I will not even wish that Peg's pubic hair would grow internally until it chokes her to death. Maybe then the bill will disappear. Or with a little luck, maybe I will disappear.

Desperately,
Adrianne

October 2, 1972

Andrew,

Tonight when Scott came back from visiting with you, he had an interesting bit of news. Peg has her hospital date set for a hysterectomy. Scott was smiling when he announced that there would not be another Helman to carry on the name. I, too, smiled because I knew that my children were safe. The red pins had done their work. The doll was exactly as I had known it would be. I could not hate either you or Peg enough to destroy you physically, but I will destroy your dreams and the immortality you and she would have had in a child.

Love,
Adrianne

October 8, 1972

Dear Andrew,

Hysterical is the only way that I can describe Leslie's state of mind when I got home. She had been crying for over an hour. I don't know what you said to her in your office at Norton Elementary School, and I don't think I want to know. It must have been the final blow to an already frustrated daughter. She said that she slammed your office door so hard that the glass rattled. When she got out to her car, she hit the car in front of her and the one behind her because she was in such a hurry to get away from you. It is a wonder she got home without an automobile accident. You never should have let her leave your office in that frame of mind.

She said that you don't love her, you don't understand her, and that Peg and the stepchildren mean more to you than she does. Leslie never wants to see you again. I tried to tell you that you were pushing too hard. Was Leslie's acceptance of Peg worth losing Leslie over? I have called my lawyer, and you will get a letter stating that you are to make no effort to get in touch with Leslie. She is old enough to make this decision. She does not want to see you. I hope in time she will change her mind but I rather doubt it. You have hurt her very deeply, and I think that she would rather face the future without any father than with one who put everyone else first. I hope that every time you look at that ugly stepdaughter you will feel guilty over how you have hurt our beautiful daughter. Someday you will pay for all the pain you have caused. I live in great anticipation of that time.

Angrily,
Adrianne

October 15, 1972

Dear Andrew,

The loneliness is surrounding and suffocating me. I can sit in one spot and feel myself fraying away. I don't know which direction to go. I am supposed to be an intelligent, responsible adult with five years of college, and now I find myself in a situation that seems impossible. I don't want to be depressed. I don't want to be sad and miserable but how do I stop? It has to come from within me but what turns on happiness?

I know that I have the best part of the divorce. I have the children. I have an important job teaching English to young people. There are a lot of things going for me. I know this, and I try to focus on them but the zombie-like feeling of nothingness creeps into my very being. All of my lifetime beliefs, goals, ambitions, and dreams have been destroyed, and I don't know how to replace them.

This is not the time to make major decisions because I am too confused. At the same time, I can't just stay in this environment of nothingness. One minute I want to apply for a teaching job in Australia, and the next minute I don't even want to teach. I want to be with the children. At the same time I resent the total responsibility of keeping them on the right track. On one hand I am free of marriage and on the other hand I am engulfed in responsibilities I don't want.

I am tired of cars that won't start, bills that won't end, decisions that have to be made, and an empty life that goes on without relief. Something has to change. I know I have to change it but I don't know how to begin. When you're forty, how do you start a new way of life with no one to help you? I hope you find happiness. I would hate to think that after all this, we would both be miserable. I feel like an amnesia victim. My past is wiped out. I am left with all the questions of: "Who am I? Where do I belong? Where am I going? Why am I here?" There are so many questions and so few answers. Will I ever be a person again?

Unhappily,
Adrianne

October 17, 1972

Dear Andrew,

I am slowly retreating into a fantasy world. I have come to the conclusion that imagination has it over reality any day in the week. I used to dream that you would come back and that some way it had been a terrible mistake. Now I realize that fantasy is a waste of dream power. Since the academic and professional world let me down, I have decided that the answer for me is to find a truck driver. If a waitress can be the answer for you, then how could I miss with a burly truck driver?

When I get a little more brave or brazen, I am going to start hanging around the local truck stop to see what passes by. I thought I might start out slowly by flirting with the driver of a pickup truck. If he turned out to be exciting as a conversationalist, I might move on to the driver of a milk truck or a mail truck. I might even consider the rugged advances of a coal truck driver. The driver might turn out to be a diamond in the rough. After all, diamonds are a girl's best friend. A diamond is only a piece of coal that has been under pressure. Surely I could supply the needed pressure if he had the coal nuggets.

For local color or excitement, I might drop by the nearest fire station and check out the driver of the hook-and-ladder truck. There would be a man who lived dangerously. That might not work because I am looking for someone to light my fire and as a dedicated fireman he might be obligated to put it out. The last thing I need is a drip or a washout.

The highlight of my fantasy comes when I picture the action involved in meeting my first semi-truck driver. That would be the ultimate. If I could be at the truck stop when one of the drivers got in from a long haul from Nome, Alaska, I am sure he would not be able to resist me. I guess if I am going to go truckin' through the rest of my life, it wouldn't hurt to have a real truck driver along for the ride.

I keep telling myself that there is a lot of mileage left in this chassis of mine but it is difficult to believe. Until I find the confidence to flirt with anyone, it is going to be a long uphill drive. I wish with all my heart that I could rev up my motor and barrel into the thick of things. But with you out of my life, my spark plugs don't ignite. I wish you would stop by and overhaul my motor. This old framework seems to be completely lost without your tender maintenance.

Love,
Adrianne

October 20, 1972

Dear Andrew,

The last few days have been more frightening. I'm in a situation that is difficult to describe. For some strange reason, I can't stand to be in my classroom. I start to get the students ready for an assignment, and it seems as if everything is closing in on me. I don't know what to say to my students.

It seems like there is extreme tension. It is like being in the middle of a crowd and suddenly everyone pushes against you, and you are trapped. I have difficulty getting my breath. I have to get out of the classroom. I can't stand to have all those students' eyes looking at me.

Talking to my classes has always been a delightful experience, now it is torture. I keep thinking that because I am a failure as a wife and as a person, I must be a failure as a teacher. I don't have any reason for teaching. How will I be able to help students prepare for life? I have not been able to handle my life situation, so how can I work with them? I am afraid that since I have messed up my life that I will mess up their lives. They look to me for answers and I don't have any answers. I feel that I have let them down. I used to live the life that I taught. Now it is all so different. It frightens me.

I need to get myself together. My teaching job is all that I have left. I have to be able to cope with the classroom situation. Teaching is the only thing that keeps me going. If I give up on the classroom situation, I know that I will give up on everything. If only you were here to help. The loneliness is awesome.

Love,
Adrianne

October 31, 1972

Dear Andrew,

You missed a fun-filled evening of family living. Scott and Leslie were in the best spirits that I have seen them in for a long time. It was contagious because they had me laughing and feeling good. We went out for a pizza and started clowning around. It was a carefree time for the three of us. We finally decided that since it was Halloween that we were going to come back home and dress up in Halloween costumes. Then we were going to drive over to the house on Maryland Trail and ring the bell. Scott was going to dress as a tramp, Leslie was going to be a large rabbit, and of course, I was going to be the friendly neighborhood witch. The three of us figured that if you couldn't penetrate our clever costumes that we could safely trick you. After all you tricked the three of us pretty good.

We had it all decided. There was one trick that would really upset you. No, we were not going to get together and flip you the bird. We had something better in mind. We know how you always hated to scrape dried egg off of the cedar siding of the house. Therefore we decided to each take a side and cut loose with a barrage of eggs. We figured if we moved fast we could have three sides in pretty bad shape. Then we could sit back and laugh while you got out your wire brush and your extension ladders. It would take you quite awhile to remove the eggs.

It doesn't take a lot to entertain us. All we have to do is picture a little misery for you, and we feel a lot better. I guess we are passing by the stage of being sorry for you. Now we would like to see you become as miserable as we are. This must be how vendettas begin. Sometimes I think that you may be as miserable as we are. Surely there must be times when you realize what you have become. It must be difficult to look in the mirror and face yourself.

If ghosts walk on this night of nights, I hope they disturb you greatly.

Spookily,
Adrianne

November 10, 1972

Dear Andrew,

Suicide as a way of ending this nightmare of personal loneliness keeps coming into my mind. Poison, guns, or turning on the gas is not the answer. Maybe if I crawled inside a large plastic trash bag and fastened it shut from the inside, I might die quickly. It would be a neat, quiet way of getting rid of myself. It would be a pre-packaged corpse. Then I think of being closed in, and I know that I would claw my way out before I died. There really doesn't seem to be a rational way to die. I suppose I find all the bad points because I'm not ready to give up on life.

These death fantasies must make me see life is better than nothing. But then life seems like nothing so where am I? This must be limbo or purgatory. I have to get a grip on myself. If I go on thinking these horrible thoughts about death I am going to break under the strain. Is there a chance that I am already insane? How would I know? Where does sanity become insanity?

I think that you should have taken out a contract on my life instead of divorcing me. There is no place in the modern society for an unwanted and discarded wife. A divorced woman on an afternoon soap opera may seem dangerously romantic but in real life she is a pretty sad specimen. Even in the twentieth century, the stigma of divorce is still there. People always think there is something wrong with the woman when a marriage ends in divorce. Society reacts with the attitude that she blew her marriage so let her work it out. It is a polite way of saying, ignore her and maybe she will disappear. I would gladly disappear if it could only be that easy. Instead I am here.

I hope that in some small way I haunt you for the rest of your life.

Love,
Adrianne

November 15, 1972

Dear Andrew,

I wish that I could write and tell you that things are going better for me but it would only be a lie. On a day that you have a hard-boiled egg for lunch and break a tooth, you can't say that things are going better. The dentist worked me in after school to the tune of a one hundred and sixty-five dollar gold cap. No, things are not getting better, only more expensive.

If you ever have a desire to kiss a girl with an expensive mouth, call me. That gold cap should put me in a special category. I can honestly say that I not only miss you but at this point I desperately miss your salary. Bring your paycheck and come home.

Love,
Adrianne

November 23, 1972

Dear Andrew,

Scott has been home every weekend since he left for Fenton College. His interest in antiques is becoming more important to him than attending college. This weekend he told me that he was planning to finish the semester at Fenton and then he was going to transfer back to Mason State. I am not surprised at his decision. I tried to tell him this summer that he would be better off at Mason State because his friends would be here. He had to find out for himself. I am glad that he had a chance to see what living away from his hometown was like. I am sorry that college turned out to be a disappointment. He was expecting a super intellectual world. College is simply advanced high school with very little room for real creativity.

Education talks a great deal about creativity, orginality, and individual effort but college boils down to meeting standard levels of busywork and passing tests over meaningless material. A college education doesn't prove intelligence, only perseverance. I think Scott realized that he might as well be in Middletown doing busywork for Mason State College. At least he would have time for his first love which I believe will always be antiques. After making all A's since he entered junior high school, I imagine now he is going to let down on the books and live a little. I'm glad that his scholarship will transfer. At least it will make it a little easier on you.

I think Scott was surprised that I wasn't upset because

he would be leaving Fenton College. That is one good point that I have gained from the divorce. There is very little that really upsets me or disturbs me. I know that regardless of what traumatic changes take place, life manages to go on and on and on. I am glad that he will be back in Middletown. Now I won't have to worry about the weekend driving. I was always afraid that he would be in a hurry and become a traffic statistic. I told Scott that he should plan on telling you of his decision. Scott says that he will tell you after it is too late to change it. He doesn't want to be hassled by your fatherly advice.

Last weekend when he stopped by to see you, he was hurt that you could put up a basketball goal, a new fence, buy bicycles for the stepchildren and Peg, but not be able to send his book money on time. Somehow your telling him that you were a little short did not impress him. Scott manages through the visits on Maryland Trail, but don't you think that once in awhile you might take him out for a cup of coffee or a meal? There is no way that he can talk to you with Peg playing the doting stepmother. Scott gets very tired of her limited range of conversation. He is glad that she was great as a waitress. He is not impressed. I think she is on dangerous ground when she talks about how happy her homosexual brother is because he has an understanding wife. Scott finds her tolerance of homosexuals and her intolerance of blacks hard to reconcile. He has a number of friends who are black so he gets tired of having her put blacks down. You better curb Peg's tongue. If some of her comments get back to the black community, your house will be number one for a firebomb contest. I don't know why I continue to worry about you. You have made it very plain that you don't need any of my suggestions. I guess after so many years I have gotten into the bad habit of worrying about you whether you deserve it or not.

Fondly,
Adrianne

Dear Andrew,

We have been divorced for almost a year. No one has swept me off my feet in a whirlwind moment of passionate madness. No one has offered me a fantastic job that would take me to romantic places. No one has found me sexy, stimulating, exciting, interesting, or even worth calling to sell a burial plot. I have changed toothpastes, deodorants, mouth washes, detergents, sanitary napkins, and my underwear. No one has noticed.

After reading a number of books on improving my mind, body, outlook, personality, and sexual potential, I am still alone. Most of the books stress the importance of being busy and productive. I keep trying. Last night I counted the number of navy beans in a pound. I was amazed that I could count them correctly the first time. I know I got them correct the first time because it was the same number I got when I counted them the second time and the third time.

The night before, I got really excited about counting the number of revolutions on a record. By moving quickly and using a stop watch I discovered that a 33⅓ record really did revolve 33⅓ times per minute. Always, before, I thought it was something that someone had made up. I checked out a couple of 78's and a few 45's. This kept me busy but I had to give it up because I kept getting dizzy.

This evening I decided that I would have to do something more intellectually challenging. I took the front page of the newspaper and counted the number of times they had used each one of the vowels. I was very systematic about it. I made a column for *a, e, i, o,* and *u.* Then I kept a tally on each letter as I went through the lines, one by one. The letter *e* is very popular in our language.

Now you have to admit that these things keep me busy. I do qualify on one potential. The one that stumps me is being productive. I don't really know how to be productive as a divorcee. My opportunities for having children are drastically reduced so it must be some kind of productivity. I started giving more assignments to my English classes and I did wind up grading more papers but that seemed like a rather frustrating way to be productive. I guess I could start growing silkworms or mushrooms in the basement for profit.

I had thought about selling Avon but I understand your new wife has cornered the market. Only a short time ago you vowed that you would work nights in a gas station rather than have her work again. Little Peg was too precious for the agonies of the working world. Maybe selling Avon doesn't count as work. All I can say is that she'd better not ding-dong my door bell, or she will be wearing her professional hat somewhere in the vicinity of her tonsils. Maybe productivity would include punching her out. That type of productivity I wouldn't mind at all. To think there was a time when I was nonviolent. Now I am spoiling for a fight. I wonder if I am too old to take up boxing as a profession. When it comes right down to it, I am getting too old for even the oldest profession. Well, maybe there are a few good years if I get the right offers. What do I mean, right offers? At this point any offer is the right offer.

The night is young, I guess I will go ahead and count the vowels on the second page of the newspaper. You never know when statistics like that would be useful in the average conversation.

Love,
Adrianne

December 12, 1972

Dear Andrew,
Never have I considered myself as a fastidious housekeeper but lately I have reached an all-time low. First, I rationalized that if the vacuum could take up a fourth of an inch of dirt, it could easily take up half an inch of dirt. From there I was only a few weeks away from checking to see if it could take up an inch of crumbs, dog hair, and

general household fuzz. It did pretty well. I figured if that type of logic would work with the floor dirt, it would work with all varieties of local household dirt. In other words, I gave up on the housework.

No one ever came to see me so it did not seem to matter whether I did the housework or not. From general apathy I moved to studied carelessness. It became a game to see who would break first, Leslie or myself. The only person who came to the house was Mark. I thought that if I did not do the housework she would do it so that Mark would not be embarrassed. It did not bother her or Mark one bit. This was even worse for me. If no one cared, why should I? Things got even worse.

I can't imagine how I used to teach school, cook meals, grocery shop, and clean house while I was married. Now I come home from school and I am totally exhausted. Even if I wanted to clean up the mess, I would not have the energy. Since the divorce I feel like I have aged some thirty years. Without you as a reason for doing things, I don't get anything done. Women need men to motivate them. You may have been only an audience but you were a needed one. Without a reason for doing, I have stopped doing. I should be ashamed of the way that this place looks but I don't seem to care enough about anything to even be ashamed.

Love,
Adrianne

December 19, 1972

Dear Andrew,

It makes absolutely no sense, but I find myself afraid to take a bath. I put it off as long as possible, and then I panic when I get in the tub. I don't think am afraid of going down the drain but I have this irrational fear of being in a tub of water. For years I used to take a bath when I couldn't think of anything else to do. A brimming tub of hot water and bubbles was an event to be enjoyed. Now it scares me.

I won't take a bath unless someone else is in the house. It is ridiculous to behave this way. I have this unspoken fear of a tub of water. I am not afraid of slipping and falling. I don't think I am afraid of drowning. It is a kind of nameless terror that creeps over me when I realize that I can't go another day without taking a bath.

It is things like this that make me think I am flaking off. What rational person is afraid of taking a bath? Why should experiencing a divorce turn me against bathing in a tub? There is no way that I am able to understand this fear. Yet, each time I need to take a bath, I experience this strange overpowering feeling of fear. I go ahead and take the bath as long as someone is in the house but it is a stupid fixation. It is so stupid that I don't even want to tell anyone about it.

If I were afraid of not taking a bath, or if I suddenly developed an obsession for taking one bath after another I would think that it was Freudian. Under the circumstances I could understand it if I believed that our relationship had degenerated to a dirty mess. Then I could cope with trying to wash away some kind of feeling of guilt because of your sexual abnormalities. Excessive cleanliness I could understand. This simple fear of bathing confuses me. I know there must be some explanation but I can't find it on my own. I am not afraid of washing dishes or of drinking water. Why should bathing in a bathtub suddenly take on the proportions of a living nightmare?

Women who become divorced must also become demented. No rational or normal person would experience the nameless terrors that fill my thoughts. It seems like I am suddenly afraid of so many things that I never even used to think about for more than a few seconds at a time.

I guess I will have to buy me some water wings for when I take a bath. Better yet, would you like to come over and be my lifeguard?

Insanely,
Adrianne

83

Merry Christmas, Andrew,

"Not a creature was stirring, not even a mouse." Everything is so quiet that I can hardly believe it. I wanted to forget Christmas but Leslie wanted the tree, mistletoe, packages, and stockings. I am glad I agreed. Christmas is always beautiful. So now she is asleep, and I am remembering all the Christmas days that we shared as a family in the past. A Christmas tree is a bundle of memories. The styrofoam star on top looks terrible. It is covered with sequins and is getting quite old. Scott made it for his second Christmas, and we have always placed it on top of the tree. So many of the ornaments were made by the children. They represent so many moments of love. The round gold lights were added for the first Christmas that we shared on Maryland Trail. So many ornaments, so many Christmas trees, and so many memories, it makes me hate being alone.

In a way I'm not alone tonight. No one can take away the memories of Christmas times that we shared as a family. All the excitement of last-minute packages, the fun of filling stockings, the wonder in Scott's and Leslie's eyes when they came out to see what Santa had left for them. There is a lot of love in Christmas, and I think that is what I will remember tonight. I will try to remember all the wonderful times we have shared as a family at Chrismas. Then maybe I will forget the fact that Christmas without a husband and a father for my children is not the same. Today as a family we had all the ingredients to make a happy Christmas, and I think we all tried to make it special for the other members but we all knew that the special love we shared with you was missing. There was simply no way to replace that.

The snow has covered everything outside. The stars are strangely bright. Maybe you too are awake and remembering past Christmases we have shared. If you are, I hope you know that I still send you a very wonderful gift of love. Somehow, regardless of what has happened, I think I will always be a little bit in love with you. Merry Christmas, Andrew. I miss you.

Love,
Adrianne

January 5, 1973

Dear Andrew,

Sometimes your son's idea of humor is beyond my understanding. He knows that Peg and you are both bigots. Even though you are the principal of an integrated school you are suddenly very anti-black. Your new wife manages to bring something about blacks into the conversation whenever Scott goes over there for a visit. Whatever she says is the old anti-Negro stereotype condemnation. Scott knows this and yet he took Candy along.

It was hard for me to believe the conversation that took place at your house. Candy and Scott came back here and thought it was hysterically funny. It seems that you and Peg walked right into the conversation that Scott had planned. You were sitting there condemning the fact that blacks and whites were dating. You foretold all kinds of problems that would result from mixing the races. Peg was very open in condemning any girl who would date a "nigger." That kind of girl would be "no-good white trash."

I wonder what would have happened if you had both known that the father of Candy's baby was a black. Candy only has about two months before the baby is due. Candy and Scott figure the baby will look black and then they are going to visit you both to hear your comments. I sometimes am not able to understand the new generation. My humor is warped, but theirs is a little frightening. I am surprised that Candy and Scott could sit there and not comment while you and Peg raved on. Maybe seeing your faces when they walk in with the baby will make it worthwhile. It's Scott's way of hurting back so I will try not to judge him. Still, I don't like what is happening to him. I talk to him but your actions have made a deeper impression than all my words.

Scott and Candy are good friends. I hope she doesn't get hurt by his humor. Candy is quite a mature young woman. She is not going to marry the father of her baby. She does plan to keep the baby. She is lucky that she has so many friends to help her. That's one thing I will admire about my son's generation, they are completely unselfish in accepting friends as they are. They don't judge. They don't condemn. They are simply there to help each other. I wish I could develop a circle of friends that I could rely on the way these young people rely on each other. I hope someday things will work out for me.

Love,
Adrianne

January 11, 1973

Dear Andrew,

All the way to school this morning, the car stalled. It would die completely and stop. Then I would restart it, and it would drive for a little bit more. I was afraid that I would never make it to school. I finally arrived in the parking lot but I was a nervous wreck. When I got to the teacher's lounge for a cup of coffee, I took a survey of the men teachers to see who could diagnose the current car illness. Everyone had a different reason as to why it kept stopping.

The teacher of auto mechanics eventually got the message that I was hinting for help. He said he would look at it right after school. I was glad because I could not picture trying to drive it back to Middletown if it continued to stall. The worst trouble about asking one of the men teachers to help is the way they always manage to hint that it is not the car but the driver of the car who has the problem. They may be right.

After school the delightful car stopped three times

from the back of the school to the side of the school where the auto mechanics teacher was waiting. He got in and drove around and around and around the school building. The car didn't even hint that it had hiccoughs, let alone anything so drastic as a chronic case of the stalls. Eventually, the teacher got dizzy so he reversed and drove around and around and around the building in the opposite direction. The motor did its best impression of a new Rolls Royce. The auto mechanics teacher finally gave up. He said it must have been cold or a bit of bad gas. I told him that my car would act up as soon as I started toward Middletown. By then he just smiled and waved his hand. That's the standard gesture of contempt for the woman driver.

The auto mechanics teacher went back into his safe secure shop. The automobile and I started toward Middletown. It gave an amazing performance of a supercar until I turned off the road that led away from school. Once it was out of sight it began to sound strange. I had not driven very far when it promptly died. I restarted it and drove on, telling myself this was not really happening to me. All the way back to Middletown it kept going more and more slowly until it would stop. By then I knew something had to be wrong with it. This was more than my imagination.

I pulled into my nearest neighborhood friendly filling station. The mechanic is very used to seeing me. I told him what had happened, and he said it sounded like a clogged fuel filter. So he took the car in and removed the fuel filter. Then he went into all the contortions, leaping in the air, and shouting that always accompanies the work that he does on my car. This time all the action meant that the fuel filter was not clogged, it was sealed off completely. Fuel could not get through the filter. All he could say was: "How could you drive it with a completely clogged filter?" I really didn't have the answer. I was only thankful that I did it. Once in a while somebody watches out for me, even if it isn't the auto mechanics teacher from school. I couldn't help but wonder why he didn't recognize a clogged fuel filter.

As an English teacher I would recognize a clogged verb in a sentence if the auto mechanics teacher had difficulty with language. It had a happy ending, so I won't push my luck. I'll bet you could unclog my fuel filter if you really put your mind to it.

Love,
Adrianne

January 28, 1973

Dear Andrew,

Leslie will never grow up. She still dreams about whatever has been exciting her or upsetting her during the day. I was sound asleep when I heard her. I thought she was calling me but instead she was only moaning, groaning, and screaming in her sleep. I hurried to her bedroom, and she was sitting up in bed beating at her feet and legs saying that the ants were eating her alive.

At two o'clock in the morning there is always the temptation to tell whatever is eating her alive to finish the job and keep me out of it. But mothers never operate that way. So I shook her and called her until she woke up. It seems that Leslie had watched a movie about the ants overrunning a whole plantation. They ate everything in sight. She was dreaming that the same ants were crawling up the bed and onto her feet and legs. She was trying to beat them off before they ate her alive. I felt sorry for her because they must have been part of a terrible dream. Once she was awake she was fine. She soon went back to sleep.

That's the way it always happens. Leslie goes back to sleep and gets her rest, and I am back at the typewriter. When something like this happens it reminds me of when she was a little girl. If she was out catching frogs, she would spend the night hopping around her bed trying to catch the frogs in her dreams. If she had played with her pet hamster, she would be crawling around under the covers

88

looking for Susie. Her dream life must be as active as her day life. Mark has quite a night life ahead of him if they decide to get married.

It is funny but I don't seem to dream anymore. That may be a good sign. When we first separated I used to dream about you and then when I would wake up I would feel so lonely because you were not there. Now that I think about it, I haven't dreamed about you since your birthday. I guess subconsciously I no longer want to be in your arms. I am repulsed by your new way of life.

Sometimes I wonder if I really loved you or if I loved the knowledge that being married to you meant that life would move in a predictable manner. Marriage may have been a protection against the unknown. If so, it was wrong. To be alive, you have to be willing to accept the unknown. I find myself wondering if there really is such a mysterious element in life as love. It doesn't seem like love should end if it is true love. What if we spent eighteen years without true love? What if I spend the next eighteen years without any love? That frightens me. No wonder I can't go back to sleep. Whatever is eating away at me is worse than all the united ants of Leslie's dreams.

Love,
Adrianne

February 5, 1973

Dear Andrew,

Maybe you did not remember that this was the first anniversary of our divorce, but I did. I am sitting here looking at a seven hundred and fifty dollar diamond, alexandrite, and sapphire pendant that I bought myself in honor of this momentous anniversary. Yes, I have slipped a cog. I must be nuts to spend money like that. Of course, that is the appraised value. I didn't pay that much for it.

Somehow I couldn't face the thought of being alone today so I skipped school. Yes, even teachers play hookey one in awhile. There was a big estate auction at Lighted Lanes near Fort Brad. So I called mother last night and told her that Scott and I would be going to Fort Brad for the auction. I thought she might want to meet us there and spend the day. The crazy woman agreed. So she is playing hookey from work.

Scott and I left before it was light, so we got up there by eight. We wanted to be able to look at all the merchandise before the auction actually started. I told Mother and Scott that I only came up to buy the diamonds but they thought I was kidding. As a matter of fact, when I said it I *was* kidding. Then a strange thing happened. The auction had advertised that the diamonds would be sold at six-thirty. Instead, they put them up for bid around noon. I had looked at them and at the bank appraisals that came with them. So I did bid on them. I was really surprised when I got the pendant for three hundred and fifty dollars. It's a good investment, and besides, I liked it. What's the use of being divorced and alone if once in awhile you don't indulge yourself? The money is all going anyway, and at least this will be something that I can leave the children when I go to a far, far better place.

I guess these are the good times. I never received jewelry like this when we were married. This ought to brighten up my life a little. Diamonds are a girl's best friend, so now I have a best friend. It doesn't replace a friendly-type husband but it was the kind of wild crazy thing that I have always wanted to do.

Scott got a lot of good buys for the shop, so it was a successful day for all of us. Mother came back with us and is going to stay for the weekend so at least I won't be alone. Possibly she and I can hit a few auctions on Friday and Saturday. At least when I am at an auction I think of something besides being alone.

Happy Anniversary,
Adrianne

Dear Andrew,   February 12, 1973

Being the only divorced woman on a high school faculty means either curling up from loneliness or developing a sense of humor. I am not sure which I do consistently. All of the secure married people have the archaic notion that the life of a divorcee is one mad fantastic whirl of sex and excitement. I must admit that if the frustrations of bringing up two young adults qualify, I do have excitement. As for that other three-letter word, I think I may have forgotten a working definition.

One of my fellow teachers, Jim Benton, offered to manage my after-school affairs if I would consent to having them for a business opportunity. Since I have almost reached the stage where I am looking for advertisement to see if our city has a paid escort service, I decided that if he could find me any after-school affairs I would consider them a business or a pleasure. I was no longer particular. Jim said he would not mind acting as my pimp for a commission on one thousand dollars a night. Believe me, I did not hesitate one minute! I assured him that for a thousand a night he could have his twenty percent starting immediately. Jim started to back off and suddenly realized that a setup like that would beat teaching all to hell.

When I went back into my classroom, he was still figuring that if one girl would bring in two hundred, a string of girls could give him the life-style he had always dreamed about. It goes to show that even securely married teachers have fantasy lives that take them out of the classroom. I hated to go back and tell him that a call girl in Middletown, Indiana, would have few offers of a thousand a night. Why discourage him? He's an enterprising teacher. If he finds the market, I've got the body—a little old, a little heavy, but willing! Oh, Andrew, see what fantasies you have reduced me to dreaming. When does normality give me a perspective on my future?

                                        Questioningly,
                                        Adrianne

91

February 16, 1973

Dear Andrew,

There are times when I know that I have to get out of the house. So instead of staring into space or at my favorite ceiling crack or doing busy work, I force myself to get dressed and get out. Tonight I went out for supper. Leslie had plans with Mark. I couldn't stand being home alone. Sometimes the memories close in and I can't get my breath. Then I run.

I decided to get a hot dog at the Mall. Not very exciting, but I have always been a hot dog freak. That lowly hot dog has come a long way. I remember, when I was a little girl, it used to be a big treat to get a Coney Island hot dog with chili sauce and lots of onions. It cost all of five cents. Tonight that same Coney dog cost me seventy-five cents. I can't believe that it tasted seventy cents better.

When I get a hot dog at the Mall, I can sit and watch the people walking in the Mall. I have always been a people watcher. People are interesting to look at as they walk by. It's kind of fun to see how various people look and how they are dressed. Some people have a natural zest for living. They almost dance along with a smile on their faces. Other people look so sad that I want to walk over and say, "Hey, do you want to talk? I'll listen." I wonder how many lonely people there are in the world. I bet it is a frightening number. Instead of our government sending rockets to the moon we should be sending out invitations to all the lonely people to come and get together. I know how they feel. I am lonely too. I wish someone would send me an invitation to go somewhere and do something. Eating out alone is not much fun. I think I even miss cooking meals for you. Come home, and I'll be the dessert.

Love,
Adrianne

Dear Andrew,

I feel like the wicked witch of the west. Part of the fun of teaching the new Phase Elective English classes is the fact that I am teaching most of the offbeat classes. I think my favorite one is called Witches, Warlocks, and Other Weirdos. I can't decide if I qualify as the witch or the weirdo. Most of the time I think my students refer to me as the witch but they always misspell the word by starting it with a b instead of a w.

The class is quite interesting. As a group they read a great many stories about witches, ghosts, and supernatural beings. I particularly enjoy the special reports that they give in front of the class. We have several reports on extra-sensory perception. The students find those very interesting. As a group we do some experiments, and it is interesting to note the number of students who do score quite high on some of the test card situations. Considering the fact that in the classroom there are very unscientific conditions, I am always a little baffled by some of the results.

There is always some time during the class for students to tell about personal experiences that they think they have had with the supernatural. I know there are forces that modern man has never tapped or understood, and I am not sure that I want to tap or understand them. The area is very touchy. I plan to deal mostly with fiction as far as the class is concerned. In real life I don't like to think how many times I have known the ending when I hear the beginning of a situation. My biggest problem is knowing that things will happen before they do but because of my twentieth-century training refusing to believe that I know. I will have to be careful with this class, or the community will be burning me for witchcraft. I am sure that it would give you great pleasure. You should hope that something happens to me before you are no longer financially responsible for the children. After Leslie reaches the age of twenty-one I may decide to remember the powers that my grandmother reserved for me. I wonder if you have ever had a strong desire to be a frog. It could be arranged.

Love,
Adrianne

March 4, 1973

Dear Andrew,

The tornado that circled my living room and left was your most unhappy son. I don't think that he understood why you suddenly decided to cut his books and expense money from one hundred and fifty dollars to one hundred dollars without any warning. Somehow I think it would have been more fatherly if you had told him ahead of time that you were going to cut his money. Arbitrarily cutting the amount of money when Scott was planning on a certain amount does not seem too fair. But then, my dear Andrew, it has been a long time since you have been concerned about what was fair, right, or ethical.

Naturally I have called my lawyer but since the agreement as to a specific amount was a little fuzzy there doesn't seem to be a great deal that I can do about the situation. There was a verbal agreement that you and Scott had but it does not seem to be binding. It is another case of, if it isn't in writing, it isn't valid. I am sorry that your son has to experience firsthand the fact that his father is no longer an honorable man.

The saddest part of the divorce is the fact that I never have to say one bad thing about you. Little by little the things that you are doing speak louder than anything I could ever say. One of these days you may expose yourself completely. I do not envy the next conversation that you will have with Scott. I will not be at all surprised if Scott is very blunt in his comments when he talks to you.

Love,
Adrianne

94

P.S.   I am sorry I was right about Scott being very blunt. I am sorry that he called you a mother f—— but he doesn't know that you're a father f——!

March 15, 1973

Dear Andrew,

Only a short note this evening, I am too tired to cope with anything. Today was one of those dreadful days. I saw one of our acquaintances from our college days. He was a professor in history. Through the years we had both taken classes from him. Dr. Ispel seemed to be pleased that he had recognized me after so many years. I wish his memory had not been so good.

He went into a glowing speech about the two of us before I could tell him that the two of us were in two separate pieces. That is always so awkward. People always seem to be genuinely shocked to discover that we are not together. As acquaintances put it: "But you two were so right for each other in every way." You must have been the world's greatest actor to convince everyone of how happy we were. You even had me convinced. I still think you must have a hormone deficiency or a brain tumor. There has to be some reason why you suddenly flipped out. Or, the awful question that keeps repeating: "Was it sudden or were you very careful through the years?" I wish you would have had the decency to tell me. Questions like that tear me up. I need to know which one of us really has the problem. What was wrong with me that caused you to change? Will I ever understand?

Poor Dr. Ispel knew that I was upset by his comments. It was one of those terrible times when the more he said, the worse it became. I finally tore myself away and hurried down the Mall trying to keep from crying. I wonder if I will ever become calloused to these situations. It always seems like these incidents tear fresh wounds in my bleeding heart.

Love,
Adrianne

March 23, 1973

Dear Andrew,

Today I said my very first four-letter word out loud. You know the word that begins with F and strikes terror in the hearts of the world? Well, I have seen it for years on bathroom walls, scrawled on desks, written in books, and painted on ceilings, but I had never said it. Today I walked into the teacher's lounge and announced that it had been a Rat F—— day. I thought that the room would crumble and the sky would open and the great principal in the heaven above would hit me with an eraser. Instead, one teacher looked up and said, "Yeh, it has been a Rat F—— day!"

There I was, letting it all hang out, being completely modern and unorthodox, and no one noticed. Times really change. Five years ago I would have blushed if I had been alone in my classroom and found it written on a desk. I think it may be difficult to become a dashing, devil-may-care divorcee in the teacher's lounge. By the time teachers have engaged in hand-to-hand combat with thirty adolescents every hour on the hour, there isn't much left that unnerves the average high school teacher.

Still, it is a sad world indeed when the basic four-letter word has lost its impact. I don't think there is anything to replace it in the English language. "Peachy darn" doesn't make it as an oral release. But then you should understand that better than I.

Love,
Adrianne

April 3, 1973

Dear Andrew,

April in Middletown is not as nostalgic as the song about April in Paris, but it does have its twinge of longing. April was the month that hinted of springtime and love-time. It was the month in which we were married. It was

96

always a beautiful month because winter melted away and the promise of warmth and wonder seemed to be ready to burst out at any second.

Where is the wonder of April for me this year? Where is the promise of something delightful that is waiting? Where is my love of yesteryear? I am filled with a mocking in my soul that makes me languish for the unknown. Somewhere up ahead in my future there has to be a bit of magic. I simply refuse to believe that I am to go on and on into bleakness. Spring is a time of promise, and I have to believe that it holds a promise even for me.

I wonder if I cast the right spell during the right phase of the moon, if I could capture all that I have lost? No, that isn't the way the magic works. The past must be buried and someday forgotten. The future lies ahead, and I am curious about what it will bring.

There was a tiny violet hiding in the grass this morning. It held the early dew. There was a beauty and freshness about it that captured my attention until I remembered an April in the rain when we gathered violets in the woods. We were so young and so much in love. I didn't pick the violet this morning but I carried the picture of it and all the violets of my life with me throughout the day. I wonder if you will notice a violet this spring? If you do, will you remember?

Love,
Adrianne

April 13, 1973

Dear Andrew,

The angel of death looked the other way this morning when I swerved to keep from hitting a dog. I drove off the road and hit a tree on the passenger side. The impact smashed the door and shattered the windshield on one side. I lost control, the car careened across the road. I could not believe that the motor was still running and that the car

97

had not turned over. There was no traffic and no one around so I didn't even stay stopped. I pulled back over on my side of the road and drove on to school. When I say I am learning to take things in my stride, I am not kidding. I got to school, parked the car, shook the glass off of my coat, and went inside. I knew the car was a mess but there wasn't anything I could do until I could call the insurance company.

I took off my coat, put my papers out to be returned, and walked down to the teacher's lounge for a cup of coffee. I think the teachers who came in after I did and who had seen my car were more upset than I was. I have reached the stage where I expect rotten things to happen. After losing you and my whole way of life, a small car accident isn't going to tear me up. The inconvenience of having it repaired will be the worst part. All the men teachers were very helpful, they thought I should have hit the dog. Men seem to be like that. Money is more important than life.

I still haven't cried or gotten upset. I am numb. That seems to be my standard reaction to everything. Numbness!

Love,
Adrianne

April 19, 1973

Dear Andrew,

This would have been our wedding anniversary. I suppose when you are divorced you should stop thinking about wedding anniversaries, birthdays, and holidays. It should be another day. Instead of that I wound up out at the local antique show. I bought another diamond. I should not be allowed out with a checkbook; I don't have any sense at all. This time I bought an antique diamond ring for three hundred and fifty dollars. It is beautiful but I have no use for it. I saw it and had this overwhelming desire to buy it. The dealer had asked four hundred and seventy five dollars for it but she gave me a dealer's discount. I am hopeful that it was a good buy. I am not sure.

Basically, I bought it to remember my wedding anniversary. I thought one of us should. I also bought it as a joke. I plan on putting aluminum foil around it so that it will fit on my little finger. Then I am going to put all my other diamonds on one hand and wear them to school. I want to see the look on the art teacher's face when she sees how badly the ring will look with aluminum foil wrapped around it. Seven diamond rings on one hand will be in very poor taste. Then I want to see and hear how she comments without being tactless. It is difficult for her to understand that sometimes I wear things in bad taste because the whole idea amuses me. Three hundred and fifty dollars may seem like a lot for a joke but I think jokes deserve to be created first class. I've got to stop doing things like this. Being divorced means being deranged. That part I can understand. At least I don't sit home all the time. Now I go out and I spend money. This too shall pass. I hope the art teacher does not disappoint me by ignoring my diamond display.

Love,
Adrianne

April 29, 1973

Dear Andrew,

It's three o'clock in the morning and I can't go back to sleep. The phone rang around midnight and it was Kathy's sister calling to say that Kathy was on the way to the hospital. The baby was on the way. Kathy wanted Leslie to be at the hospital when she went. So Leslie got dressed and I drove her out to the hospital. She was going to wait with Kathy's parents.

A few minutes ago she called to say that Kathy was fine. She was the mother of a five pound three ounce baby girl. Leslie was going to wait with Kathy's parents until they could see Kathy and the baby. Then Kathy's parents would bring Leslie home.

I guess some stories have a happy ending. Doug and Kathy are married. Doug has a job. The baby girl is here, safe and healthy. Nature is marvelous. I wish our story would have a happy ending.

Love,
Adrianne

April 30, 1973

Dear Andrew,

April is a month of memories. The memories are a mixture of pain and pleasure. This evening I had to help chaperone the annual Sadie Hawkins Dance. It is difficult for me to attend this dance because I remember the first one that we helped to chaperone. You wore your bib overalls and a loud flannel shirt. I wore a patched outfit and freckles. I came as a hefty Moonbeam McSwine. The students were delighted, and we had so much fun. You and I laughed and danced, and for a time we were as young as any of the students.

The second year you made a family of plywood pigs and painted them with smiling faces and curling tails. They are still using them as part of the decorations. It gives me a bit of a twinge to see your name on the back of the pigs where you autographed them. The decorations are similar; the music is hokey. The students are young and alive, and for a few moments I thought time had stood still. I fully expected you to come walking up to ask me to dance. So much is the same, and yet so very much is different. It was like being caught in a time wrinkle.

I am getting used to attending these things by myself but I can't honestly say that I don't miss having you there. How could we have had such good times? How could I have lived in such a fool's world? Am I still there? The memories go on and remain a part of me. You are very much in my thoughts this evening.

Love,
Adrianne

P.S. I no longer pray to understand—only to forget.

Dear Andrew,

Your birthday is a day I shall never in a thousand years ever stop remembering. I will try to forget the nightmare of finding the pictures and facing what you had become but I don't think that I ever will. I think the children had forgotten it was your birthday because they did not mention it. They may have been trying to be kind to me.

I didn't want to stay home so we decided to have an early supper at Pondabeefa. The food is usually good, and it is relatively inexpensive. I could take eating there if it weren't for the deadly routine of knowing exactly what each person is going to say as you pass from the process of ordering your steak to telling the young girl what you would like on your salad. I got to the place where she automatically asked: "And what would you like on your salad, ma'm?" I smiled and answered, "A caterpillar!" She said, "What did you say, ma'm?" I repeated very distinctly, "A caterpillar!" She never blinked or changed her tone of voice when she said: "We only have French, Italian, thousand island, and blue cheese." I couldn't resist deadpanning the comment, "Oh, really! I thought all Pondabeefa's had caterpillars!" She still refused to blink or change her tone when she replied, "Not since I have worked here." I gave up and said, "Make it French." She handed me the salad and said: "Thank you, ma'm. And what would you like on your salad, sir?" I think she was an android.

The children were nearly in hysterics, and I had a little trouble keeping my composure as we went on through the line. It has been a long time since I have felt whimsical, and we all enjoyed it. I will always wonder if the girl was smart enough to be amusing or if she was really that dumb. I may never know. I will secretly hope she was playing it straight to be humorous. Inside I have this horrible feeling that her whole life consisted of knowing four salad dressings and nothing more. The modern youth sometimes leaves a lot to be desired in terms of imagination. Anyway it was a

101

fun way to celebrate your birthday and for a little while the children and I laughed and talked and forgot about the cares of the world.

Love,
Adrianne

Dear Andrew,
Today I met Choo-Choo. Your son is dating a liberated woman. I am glad that he feels like he can drop in anytime with his friends but sometimes I wish I would have had time to swallow a cup of coffee before I meet them. Choo-Choo is something else. She is a tiny, dark-haired girl completely and totally committed to being liberated. She was wearing a short haircut equalled only by the shortness of her dress. When she sat down, I noticed that she had very long thighs for a short girl. I hope she had on a hair net or her pubic hair would be curling around the edge of her skirt. She made herself at home in one easy gesture by lighting her own cigarette. It had a pale pink wrapper. I hope it was tobacco and not a reefer. I am sure it was tobacco or at that point I probably would have inhaled and turned on.

After the initial shock wore off, Choo-Choo turned out to be as sweet as the girl next door. I try not to judge too quickly but sometimes it isn't easy being a mother. You have a tendency to believe that every girl your son brings home will be the one he marries. No wonder it is so difficult for a girl to meet a boy's mother for the first time. Choo-Choo turned out to be quite well read and an interesting conversationalist. I could have liked her if I hadn't found out that when she was not going to college; she works as a waitress. That's the word that gets me every time. Some people are gun-shy; well, I'm waitress-shy. I will try to think of Choo-Choo as a college student and ignore the fact that she is one of "those."

I enjoyed talking to Scott and Choo-Choo. It was nice to have young people in the house. I am glad he feels like he can pop in and visit when he wants. His friends are a little far out but I like them.

Love,
Adrianne

May 12, 1973

Dear Andrew,

A two-holer at the end of the path must have had some merits. At least you were not at the mercy of a plumber. Right now I'm wishing my modern plumbing hang-up was not so much a part of my life. After we moved back to Palmer Court the toilet in the small bathroom kept playing games. It would stick and run. After trying to bend, jiggle, and adjust, I gave up and tried to contact a plumber. It took five phone calls before an appointment could even be considered. Twice I set up times, rushed home, and waited to discover the plumber had had important emergencies. After two such situations, the plumber finally found Palmer Court. Then for fourteen minutes of work, he charged me $18.75. At least the toilet performed smoothly and quietly for about a month.

A few weeks ago I began hearing a mystery noise. At first I ignored it. Later I began to wonder what it could be. Finally, when Leslie admitted that she heard it, I became curious. It sounded like water running. It only lasted about thirty seconds and then it would stop. I checked the basement, the kitchen, and both bathrooms but I couldn't find evidence of anything leaking. It got so that I would sit around waiting to hear the mystery noise. I would find myself awakening in the middle of the night and hearing it. I would run around trying to find where the noise came from. I was leaning toward the theory that I had a ghost.

The mystery noise seemed to come most often from the vicinity of the small bathroom. By the time I would get there the noise would be quiet. The more I listened the more I decided that it was the sound of a half of a flush. I began to spend my spare time waiting in the little bathroom hoping it would make a noise while I was in there. After waiting and waiting, I caught it. For some reason periodically the toilet would start to flush and then stop.

This time I called a different plumber. For $24.95 he took out what the first plumber had put in the back of the tank. This took him twenty-one minutes. So for $43.70, the toilet works like it should. I don't know how long it will last but I felt a little cheated. If I had any ability as a handy person I should have been able to fix it myself. The cost of home repairs will ruin me. There is no way that I will be able to make money fast enough to repair what falls apart. I wonder if you would be interested in a part-time job. The pay is low but the fringe benefits are fantastic. I should have kept the mystery noise. At least it was friendly.

Love,
Adrianne

May 16, 1973

Dear Andrew,

I was wandering through the Mall trying to look busy when I happened to see Doris Flint's youngest daughter, Susan. Susan was feeling pretty unhappy. Susan graduated from Sushawanee about two years ago. All through high school she had gone steady with Barry Donmoyer. Barry had been in my sophomore English class and later had acted as business manager for the yearbook when I had supervised it. Barry was a special young man. I had never had Susan in class but I had known her in the halls and as the daughter of my friend. Susan had a bubbling personality and a lovely outlook on life. She made you feel good to know her. For this reason I was sorry that things were not going well for her.

Right after Barry had gone out of the area to college,

they had broken up. He was attending Purdue, and she was attending Mason State. Barry thought that since they were separated that they should date other people and have a chance to do their own thing before they became too serious. Susan had accepted this idea but she found that she was lonely without him. When we met at the Mall we both needed a friend so that we could talk. So Susan and I decided to have a pizza. While we shared the pizza, she told me all about Barry. She missed him. She knew that he was dating other girls, and it worried her. I could understand how lost and lonely she felt.

For some reason, I could honestly tell her to hold on because Barry would be back. There wasn't any doubt in my mind that they would get back together. They were right for each other. Sometimes we say those things to be kind but I really believed that things would work out for them. I knew that Barry had some growing up to do and when he was finished he would be back. I think Susan felt a little better after we had talked. It's strange. I know they will get back together. At the same time, I know that some day you will want to come back, and it will be too late. Sometimes I wish I didn't seem to know so many things. I suppose I could make a fortune with a crystal ball or some tea leaves. It is strange how there are some things that I seem to know. Time will tell which part of this is fact and which part is fancy. I do know in my heart that wanting you back and taking you back are worlds apart.

Love,
Adrianne

May 30, 1973

Dear Andrew,

This is the kind of day that I find myself not knowing whether to laugh or cry. I have been so depressed that I was even boring myself. I figured that it was time to check back with the doctor. Sometimes a timely pep talk will do wonders for a lagging spirit. Dr. Smith has been understanding throughout this whole miserable divorce. He helps me put things back into perspective so it has been worthwhile to talk to him.

When the doctor came in, I couldn't believe the change in him. He looked like he had lost twenty-five pounds and his best friend. I was not prepared to hear him tell me that his wife was suing him for a divorce. They have five children, and he thought life was beautiful. Then he went home one night and the sheriff was there with a summons. His wife was leaving him for a lawyer. She no longer loved him. There was the doctor whom I had relied on to keep me from going off the deep end, actually falling apart in front of me.

Dr. Smith had been our family doctor for a very long time so I felt great compassion and empathy for him. I came in looking for help and found that I was the one who was giving out the tired phrases of: "hang on," "in time it gets easier," "don't let it get you down," "things have a way of working out." I must be nuts. There I was giving him back the words he had given me, and I knew from firsthand experience that they were a poor excuse for the horrible agony that he was going through on the inside. There is no way that even the best words make any impression. Time is the only pain killer strong enough to make any real difference.

The only part that might have registered or helped him in any way was the fact that he knew I spoke from experience. He knew that I had walked in his experience and somehow survived. Maybe that in itself was some help.

I went in looking for answers and came out with more questions. It was difficult to believe that a divorce could happen to such a nice person. But then I am sure that many people said that about my situation. I guess the one thing you learn is that "nice" has nothing to do with divorce. I hate to think of what the doctor will be going through because he loves his wife and his children very dearly.

I think in many ways, since at least two of his children are younger than mine, it will be more difficult for him. Then again, he does come out ahead. I cheered him up and he charged me $23.00 for the office call. I think I did something wrong.

Once again I have this feeling that there is no rhyme nor reason to anything. Life is a game of chance, and some of us win and some of us lose. I am sorry that I am one of the losers.

Love,
Adrianne

June 2, 1973

Dear Andrew,

The red cap and gown were over Leslie's arm as she hurried out the door with Mark. Tonight was her graduation, and she was in a flutter of excitement. Some way there was a glow about her. She was leaving early with Mark. Mother and I were going to meet her later. I wonder if you realize that your only daughter graduates from Eastside High School this evening?

Nights like this are very difficult because they are family nights and somehow, without you, we don't have a family any more. Leslie seems like such a little girl even though she is now taller than I am. Then when she put on her cap and gown, she was suddenly all grown up I couldn't help but wonder where the years had gone.

It appears that children are a long time growing up until they reach graduation. Then all of a sudden, it seems as if their childhood didn't last any time at all. When I looked at her in her cap and gown, it was an unusual experience. Her eyes are very much like mine. Instead of a little girl looking back, I saw a young woman. Suddenly, she has grown up. You have missed a great deal this year, Andrew. The divorce has been a terrible experience for the children and for me. Leslie has been particularly upset by it. Yet as I watched her this evening, I knew that she had grown stronger by having experienced the worst of it. She is not as bitter as Scott, but she is a great deal wiser.

She did not give the valedictorian's speech or receive any of the scholarship awards like her brother, but I think in time she will be the one who becomes the success. She will do this with common sense and a loving nature. Perhaps this is more important than a super intellect. It makes a person more compassionate and more in tune with the infinite. Leslie has a quiet way of reaching out and helping when someone needs help. Instinctively, she knows the right thing to say. She is a good friend and a very loving daughter. I am proud of her tonight and every night. I hope that wherever you are tonight you can smile knowing that we did a pretty good job in bringing up our daughter.

Love,
Adrianne

June 11, 1973

Dear Andrew,

One thing about Leslie, she is determined to have her own way. She loves fried green tomato sandwiches so she has decided to grow her own tomatoes. I told her that it would be easier to buy the tomatoes but she wanted to grow her own. I think she misses the garden we had on Maryland Trail.

When I got back from the store, Leslie had bought some tomato plants. I called for her when I got in the house but she didn't answer. I went out in back, and she was in her shorts wearing one shoe. The other foot was bare. Leslie couldn't spade barefooted so she had put on one shoe. Summer for her is no shoes whenever possible. Spading with one shoe on and one shoe off is a funny sight. I watched her until she noticed me and then we both laughed.

Spading dirt is hard work but she stayed with it. It is a little late to be planting tomato plants, but she is happy about the whole idea. She got pretty good sized plants, so they should be fine. I am glad she is independent. I am too apathetic so I am glad that she goes ahead and does what she believes is important. If nothing else, divorce has been good for building her character and her confidence.

Now I wonder if she will share her fried green-tomato sandwich with me when the plants start to produce? Right now that does sound good. I hope she doesn't wind up with tomato worms. They are not my favorite type of animal life. I suppose I should have helped her dig up the ground. It is time for me to dig something. Dirt might not be the answer but it could grow into something.

Love,
Adrianne

June 20, 1973

Dear Andrew,

Utility companies are very difficult organizations to deal with because they are always right even when they are wrong. Since a month or so before the divorce, I have been trying to make the water company understand that since you no longer pay the water bill on Palmer Court, the bill should be sent in my name.

It is now one divorce and over a year later, and the Middletown Water Company is still sending me the bill in your name. I have been into the office, I have called on the phone, and I have corrected the name on the section of the bill that I send back. None of this does any good. Each month they send me the bill in your name. It seems like it would register that since the name on the check is mine, I should be entitled to the bill.

I know that it is a small matter but it irritates me. If you are out of my life forever, the water company should respect this and not keep sending me a bill in your name. I suppose that I should send it back and refuse to pay it. Or I could send it to you and then maybe they would find out it needed to be changed. With the kind of luck I have, they would probably shut off the water and then refuse to turn it on in my name.

I guess I will stop fighting it. If I ever decide to move or sell this house I can let the water bill run up to an enormous amount and then let them try to collect it from you. After all if it is in your name, why should I be a good sport and pay for it?

Love,
Adrianne

July 15, 1973
Dear Andrew,

Early this morning I had gotten dressed and packed a lunch. I had planned to meet Scott. We were going to an all-day auction at Greenvalle, Ohio. This was Leslie's eighteenth birthday, and she had made special plans to spend the day with Mark. She was looking forward to this day. As I was getting ready to leave, the phone rang. It was mother. She was calling from the hospital in Rockford.

Mother had decided to surprise us by coming to Middletown for Leslie's birthday. She surprised us. She left last night but was hit by a semi-truck. She was very fortunate to be alive. I couldn't believe that I heard her on the phone. She was bruised all over, and the doctor had taken twenty-three stitches in her head. I was very concerned so Scott and I drove to Rockford to make sure that she was going to be all right. All mother could think about was that it had happened so suddenly. It was all so unexpected. I don't suppose you really do expect to be hit by a semi-truck.

Scott and I had to go over and get her things out of the car. I couldn't believe her car when I saw it. The car looked like a giant pair of pinchers had squeezed it together. How she ever came out of it alive is beyond belief. Scott and I stayed with her for awhile. Then we made arrangements to pick her up tomorrow. I thought she should stay for a little longer to be sure she was going to be in shape to be driven back to South Benton.

It was late when I dropped Scott off and came back home. I had a very happy daughter when I walked into the house. Her birthday gift from Mark was her engagement ring. Her eighteenth birthday, her engagement, and my mother in the hospital was almost more than I could take for one day. They haven't set a wedding date yet, but soon she will be gone into the world of being an adult. I will wish her well but I will miss her deeply. I wonder what will happen when I finally wake up and realize that I am completely alone. I shudder to think about it.

Poor Leslie! Here she is engaged, and tomorrow we have to pack up and pick mother up at the hospital and take her to South Benton. It will be several days before Leslie gets to see Mark again. That's a heck of a way to start out being engaged. Her ring is lovely but not nearly as lovely as the look in her eyes. She is so very happy. I hope it lasts for her. She deserves happiness. Once again you missed a beautiful moment. You made it through the years of growing up but now you are missing the moments that make it all worthwhile. I can't believe your present way of life will ever be able to make up for what you are missing now. You have my sympathy.

Love,
Adrianne

P.S. You gave me my diamond ring on Friday the thirteenth. We thought it was daring, romantic, and exciting. The bad luck came later.

July 24, 1973

Dear Andrew,

Painting the trim on the house during the hottest month of the year was not the best idea that I ever had. As a matter of fact, it ranks right in there with some of my worst ideas. Mother is staying with us while she is recovering from the confrontation with the semi-truck. She is feeling better than all of us put together. If I get her a black snake whip, Leslie and I will have the trim painted in nothing flat.

We finally found a workable solution. We get up early and start painting around six in the morning. It is great fun to be standing on a ladder letting the paint trickle down my arm. Nothing in the world is messier than mixing me with paint. I get it everywhere. It even runs down the center of the inside of my bra. I know I am saving money by doing this myself but I wonder if it is really worth it. I suppose as a type of work therapy it does have certain merits. It is possible to be so fascinated with the monotony of painting that I don't think about anything.

I like it best of all when the yellow jackets start darting back and forth around my head. It makes me feel so wanted. One of them is going to sting me, and then I will probably fall off the ladder. My painting is fantastic. I have to admit that when I mop up the drips and dabs it looks pretty good. I am even using a special rust-resistant paint on the eaves. I may give up teaching and become a professional painter. First of all, Leslie and I took a wire brush and putty knives and scraped all the loose, flaking paint off of the trim. Then I got out the old caulking gun and fixed the windows that had lost their putty. Then we painted the wooden trim with regular outdoor white paint, and we used the special rust stuff for the eaves.

It's only a one-story house but it was quite a job for the two of us. We did give in at the peak of the eaves. Mark brought his dad's extension ladders over and did that for us. I appreciated his thoughtfulness and his hard work. I wanted to pay him but he said that it was an early birthday present for me. Basically, he is a considerate young man. I like the way he pitches in and helps out. That means a great deal to me.

The house looks a great deal better. I know the neighbors are glad that we are not letting it fall completely apart.

As painters Leslie and I made quite a team. I don't think
we are quite ready to hang out our shingles but we were
proud of our efforts. I miss your brush strokes and etcetera.

Love,
Adrianne

July 31, 1973

Dear Andrew,

Sometimes patience and silence pay off. All along I
have wanted Leslie to try one quarter of college life at
Mason State University. She has never been crazy about
school, but before she decided to settle down and marry
Mark, I thought she should give college a try. If she found
out that she didn't like it, she would not have to continue.
I felt she owed herself the chance to try. She met Mark
when you left, and I want her to be sure she loves *him*, not
the idea of being in love. If she goes to college she will have
a chance to meet other people. Then if she decides that
Mark is really the one she loves, I will feel that she is
making a more realistic decision.

We have talked briefly about it, and she knows that
I think she could be successful in the area of home economics. She has always been an excellent cook and a fine
seamstress. Put those talents with her natural ability to get
along with people, and it adds up to home economics
teacher. On the other hand, if she didn't like college, the
classes would be practical as preparation for married life.

Leslie spent the early part of the summer discovering
that jobs were very difficult to find. She is beginning to
understand that some type of extra training is important.
Today she told me that she was definitely going to try one
quarter at Mason State if I would help her. I couldn't help
hugging her with pleasure. I think she has made the right
decision. I have a feeling that Leslie is a lot more intelligent
than she has ever given herself credit for being. With a
straight-A student for a brother, I don't think she ever
wanted to compete.

We got busy right away to get her enrolled. Bless the pointed head of her guidance counselor at Eastside High School. He was all tact and consideration when he told her that with her S.A.T. scores she didn't have much chance to be successful at college work. Fortunately, that type of attitude made her more determined than ever to give college a try. It might have been the best comment he could have made. Keep your fingers crossed, Andrew. Child number two is on her way to college.

Love,
Adrianne

August 3, 1973

Dear Andrew,

For quite a while I have had an idea in the back of my mind. I need an adult to communicate with once in awhile. Our family doctor is near my age and since his wife is going to divorce him, I decided that he might be interesting in something other than a medical situation. Since it was time for me to go in for my checkup, I decided to make the most of the situation.

That means I decided to wear a dress, comb my hair, rearrange my flab, put on some make-up, and even wear some perfume. In other words I was going to do my imitation of super female. I had no idea of what I might say but I figured that I could think of something while he checked my blood pressure. I knew immediately that the old line, "Haven't we met some place before?" would never do. I also discarded, "Have you read any good books lately?" I decided to hang on to, "Why don't you come up and see me sometime, big boy?" That line has to be a historical favorite for everyone. I knew that I would have to come up with something witty, sexy, and appropriate for a doctor-patient relationship. I left it to spur-of-the-moment intuition. If all else failed, I could always ask if he wanted to come over some evening and look at my X-rays.

I am glad that I didn't waste a lot of time on a fantastic way to open the conversation. The haggard doctor of a few months before had a spring in his step and a glint in his eye. The moment I saw him, I knew that someone else had already said something witty, sexy, and appropriate for a doctor-patient relationship. I smiled and asked him how things were going. That was all it took. I soon learned that he was deeply into a relationship with a lovely young thing half his age, and if he were lucky, at least a third of his intelligence. Why do I live in a world of ten women to one man? Why couldn't I have been a dumb blonde? According to the dating statistics, I should be going with a sixty-five-year-old man. Where did I go wrong? There is something wrong in this system of male-female relationships. I am glad that things are going well for Dr. Smith; he is a very fine family doctor. Still I wonder what would happen if I would date a man half my age? The world would probably shriek with disapproval. Needless to say, my blood pressure was a little high today. It was one of those times when my mood went down and my blood pressure went up. It cost me twenty-three dollars to find out that the only eligible man in Middletown was no longer eligible. There goes my dream of free penicillin! Oh, well, tomorrow is another day.

Love,
Adrianne

August 14, 1973

Dear Andrew,

Mice have never frightened me, but then I have never been on a first-name basis with them. Some way, somehow, one or more of them have moved into my life. I have never understood how a mouse decides to become a roommate, but I know that periodically it happens. I would have thought the two enormous dachshunds would have frightened them away, but Snoopy and Linus have never realized that they could frighten anything except each other.

I was reading one evening before Leslie came home from a date, and I thought I saw something dart behind the davenport. It moved so quickly that I didn't think I saw anything. Then I began to notice tiny brown calling cards in the most unlikely places. This mouse must have been a circus mouse because he was on top of everything. Mother came to spend the weekend, and I was glad because I had forgotten how to set a mousetrap without getting my fingers caught in it. We set several of them and used both cheese and peanut butter for bait. That was in case it was a gourmet mouse.

We had all gone to bed when I heard mother calling me. I thought she was sick or something. Instead she told me to listen. I listened but I did not know what I was supposed to hear. Mother informed me that the mouse was playing with a marble. I listened but I still couldn't hear anything. I got up and turned on the lights and looked around but I couldn't find any marble game with mice going on.

I went back to bed and was trying to go back to sleep when mother called me again. This time she said: "Adrianne! Adrianne, you have to do something about that mouse. I can't sleep in a house that has a mouse playing marbles." It's four in the morning, and I am supposed to break up a mouse marble game! Mother weighs two hundred and fifty pounds—why can't she put her foot down? If she put her foot down hard enough she could break up fifty marble games and a good twenty-five mice.

I got back up and turned the lights on. Where do you start looking for a mouse who is playing marbles? I pushed some of the furniture around and made a lot of noise but I still didn't find the marble game of the night. I thought about calling the vice squad from Middletown but I don't think we have any city rules that prohibit mice from playing marbles in a private home. Of course, if I could prove

116

the mice were betting on the results of the game, I might have a legitimate reason for calling. But, let's face it. I couldn't find the mice let alone their gambling money.

By this time, mother had gone back to sleep and I was wide awake. I wonder if I would call you up if you would come over. You could have your choice. You could either trap the mouse or me. Or we could sit around and play marbles. This time of the morning I am losing my marbles. One nice part about it, mother and the mouse are asleep.

Love,
Adrianne

August 21, 1973
Dear Andrew,
This experience is one you should not have missed. Scott and his antique shop partner, Jeff, share an apartment. They have had supper over here a number of times. Right along they have promised to invite me over for a meal that they would cook. This was the rare experience. They invited me for supper this evening. When I got there, they were pleased to see me. I had worn a long skirt and a frilly blouse since I knew they would dazzle me with fine silver, china, and candlelight. They were both dressed up and Jeff had invited Dollie to join us. In other words Dollie got to help cook, and I am sure that if she played her cards right, they would let her help clean up.

The table looked lovely if you could ignore the fact the dining room carpet probably had not been swept in a year. Most of the apartment was an arrangement of dirty clothes, books, and antiques waiting to be worked on when the boys had spare time. I started into the kitchen to see if I could help but when I saw dishes from the last three weeks, I decided that I would only be in the way. I wanted to concentrate on how lovely the table looked and forget about the cockroach that was walking across the buffet. Little things like that are not important when your only son invites you to dinner at his apartment for the first time.

They had fixed some kind of round steak with a tomato gravy, green beans, mashed potatoes, and a salad. They also had coffee. Scott and Jeff tried to make the dinner tasteful and attractive. I appreciated the effort. It was their way of trying to help me spend one less evening alone.

After dinner, they said they would clear the table while Dollie and I visited for a little bit. In a few minutes they joined us in the living room, and we played Monopoly. I am a little old to be on the floor playing Monopoly but I managed to last through most of the game. They were very young, alive, and full of fun. It was a pleasant way to spend an evening. I wonder if there was ever a time when I was that young, that alive, and that full of fun?

I thanked them for a lovely evening and started home. Their evening was probably only beginning. I am sure they would have other friends dropping in and would spend several more hours of laughing and having a good time. Even with the dust, the cockroaches, the clutter, and the mess, I am just a little bit jealous. It would be good to live in a do-your-own-thing world with friends who liked you because you were you. I would like to say that I will do my own thing but somehow at forty it isn't much fun. Doing your own thing means doing it alone. Forty should be husband, home, and fireside. Instead, I come home and communicate via the typewriter to a man who loves someone else—to a man who doesn't exist any more. Strange world indeed!

Love,
Adrianne

August 26, 1973

Dear Andrew,

Movies are a far cry from the days of my childhood. When I was growing up I could spend ten cents and see a double feature, a cartoon, news of the week, a serial, selected shorts, and a preview of the coming attractions. The management didn't care if I sat through it twice. Remembering

118

the good old days of my childhood, I decided to try the movies. I figured that movies in the afternoon might help me spend the long day. So Leslie and I checked out the newspapers and decided to hit the local matinee movie.

What a bummer! It cost us $1.50 each. That simply got us in the door. Next it cost us another $1.50 for two containers of popcorn and two Cokes. I am not going to say that the movie was short but I still had popcorn left when they started the coming attractions. The movie must have lasted all of an hour and thirty-five minutes. Then they had local commercials showing the building fronts of places we should patronize. For almost five dollars I had killed less than two hours. Movies in the afternoon were not the way to use up the long summer days. I could get better mileage by watching the reruns or the soap operas on television.

No wonder children don't have any imagination. The movies are not exciting, funny, or even interesting. They aren't even long!

Tomorrow is another day. Surely there will be something for me to do. I suppose I could drive by your house and flip Peg the bird but that has been done before. Maybe I could get a flat tire.

Love,
Adrianne

September 6, 1973

Dear Andrew,

Mother has been visiting for a few days. She and Scott had the great idea that we should go to an auction at Lighted Lanes. It was one of those all-day double auctions that advertised a little bit of everything to sell. The little bit of everything included a great many antiques of various kinds. We vowed that we would be very selective since the three of us were driving there in her Vega Hatchback. The auction was scheduled to start at nine in the morning.

Saturday morning could be a morning to sleep in but the location of the auction was a good two-hour drive.

Then, of course, we had to allow an hour for looking at the items before the auction started. Mother and I picked up Scott at six and started merrily on our way. There is always an element of excitement about attending an auction. You always wonder if this will be the one where you get the buy of the century. It never is, but you always dream about the opportunity.

The morning moved slowly because the auction included a great deal of broken and chipped glass. By afternoon the auctioneers were beginning to auction some of the furniture. Scott got a good buy on a drop-leaf table. I wasn't worried because that could go in the back of the car. Then he got a rocking chair. That could be taken apart so I still did not worry about transportation back to Middletown. Mother and I had accumulated numerous small items that could fit into a couple of cardboard boxes. Scott bid on a love seat. I didn't worry until he got it. While mother and I were trying to figure out how we could get all the stuff packed into the Vega, we didn't realize that Scott had picked up two more small tables and an ornate floor lamp with a large shade. I stopped him and called a council of war. There was no way to get all that stuff back to Middletown in the Vega. If we didn't stop bidding or do something it would be an impossible situation. Since there were still a great many things to be auctioned off, Mother and Scott decided to drive in to Fort Brad and see if they could find a small U-Rent.

I did not anticipate any problem so while they were gone, I bid on a couple of picture frames and a large chair with lion heads carved on the arms. It was an excellent buy, and I was quite proud of it. A short time later Mother and Scott came back. I noticed they did not look happy when I told them what I had purchased. Then they told me that the bumper of a Vega was too small to attach a U-Rent. They could not rent anything to simplify the hauling. That meant we were two hours away from Middletown with all that furniture.

We voted against driving back for a second car. Packing has always had a certain fascination for me so I decided to see what I could do. Mother had rope and padding so that was a help. First, we tied the drop-leaf table on top of the car with the legs sticking up. Then Scott took some of the tables and the rocking chair apart. We put the seat of the Vega down and put the love seat in first. Then we started packing around it. We got everything inside except for the end of the love seat, which stuck out the back. Scott tied the lid of the Hatchback down so it would not fly off in the wind. There was a very uncomfortable space in back of the passenger's seat where I would have to curl up until we got back to Middletown. It wasn't easy but I curled myself into the space. Scott started driving back, and we realized we were dying of thirst.

Before long we saw a restaurant. People were staring out the windows as this little Vega drove up with a table tied on top of it and a strange assortment of furniture sticking out the back. They stared even more when six feet of Scott got out on one side and two hundred and fifty pounds of mother got out on the other. Then someone a little shorter and not much thinner emerged from the back seat.

As I leaped forth, bent double with a cramp in my leg and back, I could tell by the astonished looks on their faces that the people in the restaurant had difficulty believing that we were real. They figured it was some kind of trick car. We got some Cokes and got back in and disappeared down the road. I bet some of those people will always wonder what we were supposed to have been. I was only sorry that we did not have a picture. It would have been a fantastic advertisement for a Vega Hatchback. No one would have believed all that we had packed in that little car if they had not been there to see it.

It was a long and miserable ride back to Middletown. I am not as flexible as I like to think I am. I was glad to get the stuff unloaded at the shop and get back to take a hot bath. I thought it would be easy to fall asleep but once again it eluded me. Even though I had spent too much money and I feel like my body is warped from the ride back, it was a good day. I enjoyed spending the day with Scott and with Mother. Somedays I find that I am almost happy without you. Those days are rare.

Love,
Adrianne

September 16, 1973

Dear Andrew,

Because Scott has been sick so much of his life, I have always told him that when he looked for a wife he should be sure that she was strong and healthy enough to pull a plow. I figured his wife would probably wind up taking care of him, so she should be physically strong. I was not quite prepared for the day that he would take me seriously. The day was today. I was cleaning up the kitchen when I heard him come in the front door. He yelled: "Mom, come on out. I want you to meet Cupcake."

I was not quite prepared to meet Cupcake. She looked like something off of the Green Bay Packer's team. Scott is a big guy but she made him look like one of the seven dwarfs. I hope my surprise didn't show as I rushed in, came to a dead stop, and stared. Cupcake seemed to be used to people staring because she smiled and said, "Hi, I'm Cupcake." I told her I was glad to meet her and then wondered if the sofa would hold her. Scott was pleased with her. I could tell that because he was wearing a hickie on his neck that was large enough to cover Chicago.

This was the type of daughter-in-law I had always dreamed about so I decided that I had better get used to her. It seems that Cupcake had stopped one day when Scott had a flat tire and couldn't get the jack to hold up his Opel. I guess Cupcake held up the side of the car while he changed the tire. One of those true-life romance kind of meetings! They started talking and discovered that they shared some of the same classes at Mason State.

With all that in common, they decided to try the date route. So far it seemed to be going quite well. They had only stopped by to pick up a few paperback books that Scott needed for a research paper.

One nice part about it, Cupcake did not work as a waitress when she was not in school. She worked at one of the gas stations near the college. As I said, a mother always looks at the girl her son brings home as the one he might marry. This one has tremendous possibilities. She is strong, sturdy, and understands automobiles. I think she could be the perfect wife for Scott. If he ever got out of line, she could break him in two.

Scott has brought home a lot of girls since the divorce, but he is bitter about the idea of marriage. That is one of the things that makes me sad. Leslie thinks marriage is the only answer. Scott thinks marriage is no answer at all. I wish they could work out a balance on their ideas. Maybe that will come later. I hope in time they both find mates who will give them a happy marriage.

Love,
Adrianne

P.S. Is there such a situation as a happy marriage? I thought I had one but I was wrong. I hope they won't be wrong. Will they learn from our divorce?

September 20, 1973

Dear Andrew,

In trying to keep myself occupied, I get into some weird situations. This evening I shook out the long black wig, hopped into a colorful long skirt and blouse, and put on all the junk jewelry I could find. I topped it off by tying a scarf around my forehead and carrying my crystal ball. Tonight I was the gypsy of the fortune-telling set. No, I have not taken on a part-time job; I was simply doing a good deed.

My neighbor Lisa Hendricks is a member of the Tulip Club. She had asked me to come some evening and pretend to tell fortunes as part of the entertainment. When I had agreed, it had seemed like a good idea. Now after teaching all day, I was a little sorry that I had agreed. But it is important for me to stay busy.

Lisa drove and we got there early. The club meets in the basement of a church. It seemed like a strange place to have a gypsy fortune-teller. Lisa tried to tell me a little bit about the people but it is the kind of club that has a lot of members but no way of knowing which ones would appear on any given evening. The club works through the church to do good deeds and community service. I knew I would never be able to remember the names, descriptions, and information so I was prepared to rely on intuition. I figured if I gave a person some vague ideas that I could pick up enough clues from her reaction to tell her something that would be believable.

There were about fifteen people there. The club members were all adults but they acted as giggly as high school girls. I had figured right for most of them. By hinting a little and then picking up on their reactions, I soon heard them saying, "Well, how did you know that?" I was pleased and it was fun. I told only good news so maybe as a morale factor it might have made their days a little brighter. I hope so. People need all the bright spots in life they can find.

I hope all the good things do come true for them. They were nice and even had a gift for me. It was a pretty scarf, and I appreciated their kindness. I had not expected a gift. I shared some of the refreshments and before long the evening ended. I was tempted to run off and become a gypsy full time, but the wig was hot and my crystal ball was a bit cloudy. It always gets that way when I look in it to see what will eventually happen to me.

Love,
Adrianne

Dear Andrew,

Talk about addiction! I have it. I got hooked on auctions and tonight if ever a person mainlined an auction, I did. It must be a type of gambling obsession that could get out of hand. I joked about it when my mother and son became fascinated by auctions. I figured it was funny when they kept attending auctions and buying. They had reasons. They were interested in antiques. I didn't realize that I had slowly moved from the status of watcher of auctions to bidder at auctions. It's like one drink leads to another: one bid leads to another.

I had been pretty sane in buying things that could be used for my son's shop or that could be put away for when Leslie set up housekeeping. Most of my purchases were rational. I prided myself on being able to stop bidding if the price got out of hand. I had seen too many people pay too much for an item because they got carried away with the excitement of bidding. There is a kind of frantic excitement that takes hold when the bidding narrows down to two people. It's this sense of excitement that becomes an addiction. They should have an Auctions Anonymous. I proved that I should join if they ever decide to develop one.

There was an auction advertised for the edge of Middletown. Most of the items were ordinary household items, but for some reason I was intrigued by a description of a couch with a set of lions for the arm rests and across the back. I have always been fascinated by lions and the description excited me. The couch was mahogany, and I seemed drawn to it. I kept thinking about it all week and finally decided to at least go to the auction and check it out. There were a lot of tools advertised so Leslie and Mark decided to meet me there. A great deal of junk had to be auctioned but I decided to wait it out because I was impressed by the lion-figured couch. It was mahogany on the sides and on the back. The bottom needed to be reupholstered but it was a truly magnificent piece of furniture.

125

I knew that I should leave but I had this uncontrollable desire to bid on this piece of furniture. I figured that I would bid a little and if the price got too high I could always stop.

It was dark by the time they got the furniture. The auctioneer's crew had strung lights up between the house and a large tree. The couch was in the center and it looked enormous and impressive. The auctioneer finally described the couch and started taking bids. The first bid was twenty-five dollars. I raised it to fifty. There was a growing tension in the crowd. I knew I should have stopped. The bidding continued and by the time it got to two hundred and fifty the contest had narrowed to one gentleman on the other side of the crowd and myself. By the time I got to three hundred and fifty dollars I was obsessed with owning that couch. Leslie and Mark both tried to talk me out of bidding any more. I wouldn't listen. I knew I had to keep bidding, and I did.

At four hundred and thirty-five the bidding stopped and I had purchased an enormous mahogany couch that needed to be refinished, reupholstered, and would in no way fit through the front door of my house. I had mainlined my first auction. I beat out the competition and could take home the merchandise. When I wrote the check I got sick inside knowing that a whim had cost me more than I could afford to spend. I had done what I had made fun of other people for having done. I had gotten caught up in the bidding and continued to bid for the sake of bidding long after a reasonable price had been passed.

I was now the owner of the most expensive used couch in Middletown. The little people of the auction were impressed. Those who had been bitten by auction fever knew they had seen a prime example of bidding madness. It was one of those rare moments of auction madness that the auction addicts remember to tell their friends about. I was now one of the loyal brotherhood of auction freaks. There are no excuses for this type of behavior. It happens to almost normal people. I only hope that someday Scott will be able to get the money out of the couch. At least it is one hell of a status symbol for the shop. Scott loved the couch but not the price tag.

I think that I had better give up attending auctions for awhile. The couch was so big that it took four men to load it into the truck. It may not be a white elephant but it comes pretty close. I only wish I had a house that would show it off. It is a wonderful piece of furniture. I was glad that the shop door was wide enough to accommodate it or I would have been in real trouble. I wonder if you would have allowed me to store it in your garage. That would be the day. For four hundred and thirty-five dollars, I could have hired a date.

Love,
Adrianne

October 10, 1973

Dear Andrew,

For a while now I thought I was getting over one of my biggest problems. This afternoon it hit me again. Buying groceries is the hardest thing for me to do. For some reason, I get in the grocery store and start to shop. The next thing I know I am crying. It is dumb and I hate it but I can't seem to control it. It hadn't happened for a long time and I thought I was getting over it. Then it happened.

So many of our evenings out were spent at the grocery store. It was something we had always done as a family. There is something about being in a grocery and seeing all the families shopping together that breaks me up completely. I see the little children sitting in the carts or I see the youngsters walking beside the cars putting in packages of cookies and things without their mothers realizing it and I cry. It brings back too many memories.

No matter what time I shop, there is always some man pushing the cart and adding up the purchases the way we used to do for so many years. You and I were so conscious of money that we always added up the items as we went along. We wanted to be sure that we did not put in more groceries than what we could pay for at the checkout counter.

I suppose there will always be times that the memories are so strong that I will respond with tears. I guess I should be glad it doesn't happen as often as it used to. I know that I am making progress. It takes time. Still there are days when I would give all my green stamps to see you for even a few minutes.

Love,
Adrianne

October 15, 1973

Dear Andrew,

This was a strange day. I had trivial phone calls from people who wanted me to consider their companies for taking the prom pictures or to hire their rock band for the prom. Sometimes the joys of being a class sponsor are endless. It is always a hassle to leave class and dash to the office for a phone call. About eleven I was coming back from a phone call, and I looked toward the front door of the school building. Mrs. Farraday was talking to the principal.

It struck me as being unusual for her to be out of her classroom at that time of day. I started to walk over to talk to them and then changed my mind and went on toward my classroom. I had this feeling that I should say something to her because it would be the last time that I would have a chance to see her again. I dismissed the thought and went on to class. Later on, I learned that she had gone home because she was ill. It made me think about not having stopped to talk to her. I wish I would have said something. I am always sorry when I have these impulses and I don't pay any attention to them.

Anyway it was a strange day and a long day. I am very tired so I think that I will shut off all my strange feelings and try to get some rest. Sleep will keep me from thinking.

Love,
Adrianne

October 18, 1973

Dear Andrew,

One of the teachers called to tell me that Elaine Farraday had passed away only a few hours earlier. She had a heart attack, and it was fatal. You can't imagine how strange I felt when I got the call. What was there about the last time I saw her that made me know it was the last time I would see her? It frightens me when these things happen. I don't really like to know the future ahead of time.

I will be rational about this. I probably have a hundred predictions that I make mentally and forget about because they don't come true. It stands to reason that I would only remember the ones that come true. I will not try to remember any of them.

The teaching profession lost a fine teacher today. Life seems to be one loss after another. I wonder if we ever understand why?

Love,
Adrianne

October 21, 1973

Dear Andrew,

Women are strange, foolish creatures. All the time that they are overworked and overinvolved because of their husband and children, they dream about a time when they will be able to do the things they always wanted to do. Freedom to a wife and mother sounds like a magic world of carefree living. I wasn't any different. I remember countless times when I thought, Well, if I didn't have diapers to wash, meals to cook, errands to run, or a thousand things waiting for me, I would be very creative, artistic, productive, and motivated. If I had the time I would certainly find rewarding activities.

Now we are divorced. The children are very self-sufficient. I have endless hours of freedom. The irony is that I can't think of a creative, artistic, productive, or motivated activity that would be nearly as rewarding as being in the middle of family living. The hectic quality of finding a lost sock, typing a late paper, or feeding six extra kids was a time to be treasured. It was a time when I was a part of something important and wonderful. At this point I have not found the compensations in the magic world of freedom.

I realize now that it was wrong for me to have been so completely concerned with being a wife and mother. Being a person should have been first. Each person has an identity and it is important that each person keeps that identity. Because my identity became wife and mother, it is very difficult for me to now become a person. I keep looking over my shoulder to see what I am forgetting. My need to be needed is greater than I care to admit. Too many things happened too suddenly, and I am slow to recover. Teaching helps but it is not the complete answer.

Love,
Adrianne

November 6, 1973

Dear Andrew,

Leslie has been a bundle of raw nerves waiting for her first set of grades to come in from Mason State. Stars were in her eyes when she received her grades and discovered that she had gotten three A's and one B. Not bad for a little girl whose counselor told her that she couldn't make the grade for college. I was so pleased for her. This has given her the biggest boost in education that she has ever had.

The one thing her guidance counselor hadn't realized

was that her S.A.T. scores might have been low because her reading speed kept her from finishing the test. Leslie reads slowly but when she is done she remembers what she has read. By putting in some extra hours Leslie has come through with flying colors. As a mother I am pleased with her. It isn't the grade that is important, it is watching Leslie discover that she is capable of successfully doing what she sets her mind to accomplish.

For years I have said Leslie was the smartest one in the bunch, but no one listened. It looks like she may prove it on her own. Once again you missed sharing the most beautiful smile in the world.

Love,
Adrianne

November 9, 1973

Dear Andrew,
The date is probably one you would not remember. Its significance didn't register with me until late this afternoon. The morning was strange. I thought I had long ago given up crying without a reason; that's why it disturbed me to notice that as the morning progressed, I grew more and more sad. Around nine-thirty I found myself crying for no reason at all. The tears simply would not stop. Leslie was upset because I was crying and I could not for the life of me give her any concrete reason as to why I was so upset. Nothing unusual had happened that might have triggered the tears. As a matter of fact, things had been going fairly well. I couldn't understand why this morning was so dismal.

Around three o'clock mother called and asked me if I knew what today was. I hadn't realized the date until she told me it was November 9. My grandmother had passed away on this day three years ago. Mother went on to explain that she had taken some flowers to my grandmother's grave at about nine-thirty this morning. I asked her if visiting the grave had made her cry, and she said yes. That must have been the reason that I was crying this morning. Someway, something had triggered sadness. Without realizing it, I was sharing a moment of grief at the same time my mother was. At least now I know that there was a subconscious reason for my behavior. Someday I am going to write down these strange coincidences and see if there is any pattern or reason why these things happen to me. Maybe my grandmother had not been joking when she said that I would be the next witch in our family. If I am, I am not very successful or surely I would have my life in better shape than it is. At least I wasn't crying over you. There should be some consolation in that.

Love,
Adrianne

November 12, 1973

Dear Andrew,

Sundays are the most difficult days. I manage to keep busy during the week because of schoolwork, after-school activities, and lesson planning or paper grading. Saturdays are acceptable because there is laundry, housework, and grocery shopping. Sundays are something else. Leslie usually has something planned with Mark, and I try not to tag along. I have been trying to look for places to go and things to do. After spending all that money on the lion-headed couch, I have tried to stay away from auctions. I can't afford to let my bidding get out of hand. I love the couch. I think it adds something to the antique shop, but I do have to be more careful and not fall into the auction pitfall of being carried away by the bidding.

I have given myself several long lectures so I decided that I could be trusted to attend an auction. I was pretty safe because I only had fifty dollars in my checking account. The newspaper had advertised an auction at the Fair-A-Day Motel in Raymont. They had several fantastic items advertised. I felt that most of the things would go too high so I could have a pleasant afternoon looking and listening. There are always people to talk to at an auction. It's a friendly place and you may always talk to the person next to you. Then, too, the one advertised today was a Clinton auction; they are always fast moving and well organized.

Leslie went out to spend the day with Mark at the farm, so I went to Raymont early enough to have lunch before the auction started. The food is excellent at the Fair-A-Day Motel dining room so I went directly there. I had a leisurely lunch and still had time to look at the display of antiques before the auction started. The auctioneers had not arrived but Nick, the setup man, was unpacking the last few items. Nick does a good job of setting the items up for display. He told me that I should be sure and notice the cloisonné lamp because it was very unusual. He was right. It was small, but it was a beauty. I was glad I got there early so that I could look closely at the various items. Several of the good things had some damage so I knew I wouldn't be tempted to bid on them.

There were several people there to whom I could talk. I don't know them by name but they are friendly. They are people who attend auctions frequently. After attending many of the same auctions that they do, you begin to feel like friends—at least you feel like friends if you don't bid on the same items.

Prices were high and stayed pretty steady for most of the auction. I bought a couple pieces of patterned glass, and I was feeling very proud that I was being reasonable. I had made a mental note to congratulate myself on not getting carried away when Clinton put the cloissonné lamp up for bid. For some reason, the bidding was slow. I knew it was too good to go cheaply so I started bidding on it. I figured there wasn't any danger because it should bring around one hundred and fifty dollars. Imagine my surprise when I got it for sixty-five dollars! I knew it was a good buy but I believe I was illegal. I was writing a check without the sufficient funds in my checking account to cover it. That meant Leslie would have to get to my bank when it opened in the morning and make a fast deposit. This is exactly the type of thing for which I yell at Scott. Then I turn right around and do it myself. Now someone will have to yell at me. That's the part that I miss most of all. No matter what dumb thing I do, there isn't anyone to notice or to yell.

I stayed for the rest of the auction to watch the prices but I controlled my impulse to buy. It made a fun afternoon, and the lamp was a good buy. When I was paying my bill and checking out, Nick came along and told me it wasn't fair for me to have stolen that lamp for only sixty-five dollars. I hoped that Scott would feel the same way. I stopped by the shop on the way back, and he did. For once, he said, I had made a good purchase. I didn't tell him about the check. Leslie will take some money out to the bank in the morning, and it should be a problem-free day.

By the time I had finished talking to Scott, the wonderful auction day was pretty well shot. I wonder what you find to do on a long Sunday afternoon. I wonder if for a short time you miss me and what used to be? I doubt it. I don't think you ever look back. I wish I could be that way.

Love,
Adrianne

November 19, 1973

Dear Andrew,

Economizing and Leslie have always been a strange combination. She has been making monthly payments on a sewing machine. The payment is ten dollars and fifty cents a month. Because of school she has been working fewer hours so she has felt the pinch. Finally, she came up with what she considered as a fantastic way to solve her problem and mine. She needed money, and I needed some plain colored dresses that would look decent for school. Her idea was to make me a dress, and then I could make her sewing machine payment.

According to her reasoning, it should be a good deal for both of us. I should have remembered I was an English major and not a business major. After buying material, pattern, inner facing, thread, zipper, and buttons, I began to wonder. When I added up the cost of all that plus the cost of the sewing machine payment, I decided that I would soon have the most expensive wardrobe in Middletown. She keeps explaining that I am getting personally fitted, exclusive dresses at a very reasonable price. What she keeps forgetting is that I ordinarily shop for sale items at Air-Mart.

Now I have to admit that she is an accomplished seamstress and the dresses that she makes are really beautiful. They fit well and I receive many compliments on them. I should be delighted, and if it were not for the expense, I would be. As it is, I think I will be glad when she works more hours and I shop at Air-Mart. I am afraid her sewing is a luxury that I can only afford during those weak wistful moments when I know that her finances are rougher than mine. Mothers are like that. We can't walk away from our responsibilities. Maybe the next time I experience reincarnation, I'll decide to be a father. It must be a lot easier than being a mother.

Love,
Adrianne

November 23, 1973

Dear Andrew,

Sometimes attending an auction is exciting. There was a very large all-day auction advertised at the fairgrounds in Oxford, Ohio. A great deal of exciting furniture was advertised, so Scott and I decided to take a chance that we would be able to pick up some furniture at a reasonable price. Scott had finished moving some furniture and the

U-Rent was still hooked on my car so we decided to take it with us. Leslie was going along. We got up bright and early. Well, anyway, we got up early and headed for Oxford, Ohio.

The drive over was pleasant, and for once Leslie and Scott were enjoying each other's company. With a brother and a sister, you never can be sure of how they will react to each other. The three of us don't often go to an auction together when it is strictly antiques. Leslie isn't that interested in antiques. She likes auctions when she can pick up something to put away for when she gets married. Anyway, we had a good time talking and laughing along the way. It was only slightly unnerving to have the empty U-Rent following along behind the car.

When we reached the fairgrounds there was already quite a crowd. I had forgotten that Ohio time was different, so that meant we had to rush a little to look at things before the auction started. It seemed like they had enough stuff for three auctions. Scott and Leslie went on to look around while I picked up a bid number and gave them my identification. I don't know why they always get so upset when I don't have any credit cards. There was a time when cash or a check was important. Now, if you don't charge it, they think you are strange. I finally showed them my driver's license and my teacher's retirement card. They decided I could have a number. I also showed them my blood donor's card and my speed reading certificate but they were not impressed by either Type A RH negative or a thousand words a minute with 99 percent comprehension. I rather thought that was a more accurate identification than my driver's license, but people are impressed by strange things. By the time I was identified and numbered, I was a little disgusted with the whole idea.

I should have been patient because I was in a foreign state and this was a different auction circle, but sometimes the business of identification is a fiasco. I am sure that if I were going to forge a check I would have had sense enough to forge all kinds of identification. I should have lived during a time period when a person's word was binding. It is a wonder I don't get taken because I am always trusting someone. I think I must have a dishonest face because I always have to show enough identification to be related to a Nixon.

I finally got in and looked at the antiques very briefly. The bidding started almost immediately and we were ready and alert. The best buys usually come at the very beginning and the very end. The auctioneer put up a silver teapot and a silver napkin ring. Scott bid and got it for twenty dollars. It was the buy we had dreamed about because the napkin ring was coin silver and worth at least thirty dollars. The little silver teapot was a real sleeper. It had all the proper markings to date it in the seventeen hundreds. It would retail at about two hundred and fifty dollars. That made the trip over worthwhile. One of the other bidders came over to see if she could buy it immediately but Scott was smart enough to hang on to it until he could check it out more fully. The fact that someone else wanted it immediately made us pretty sure that it was a good buy.

We spent the rest of the day hoping we could pick up some furniture. The prices for furniture were unreal. They seemed to get higher as each piece was auctioned. We did pick up an oil painting for ten dollars and a pretty fair piece of art glass for nine dollars. By late afternoon we were hot and we had exhausted our patience so we decided to get back to Middletown. I can't believe that we drove over with a U-Rent and bought only enough for one of us to carry out to the car. That meant driving back with that empty trailer on the back. We never seem to get it right. If we buy a lot of furniture we have mother's little Vega. If we buy a few small items we have a truck or a U-Rent. I guess the absurdity is half of the fun.

Love,
Adrianne

December 2, 1973

Dear Andrew,

The television had an advertisement for computer dating; it was a service that operated out of Indianapolis. I copied down the number. I think I will write to them and see if I would be able to find a date for myself. It could be my Christmas present to me. I figure it may take something unusual to snap me out of the doldrums into which I keep slipping.

I suppose with my luck the company would run my card through the computer and the machine would short out. Or if I punched all the information sections correctly, my card would be the only card in Indiana for which there wouldn't be anyone compatible. I don't suppose that at this time I could fill out a questionnaire and be rational about myself. I don't think that I really know what I am interested in or what I care about. The company might send me the card and I could write across the top of it: "Send warm male body."

Right now I simply need someone who is alive to talk to me. Having no one special to whom you may talk is the worst part of being divorced. There is no personal individual with whom you may establish a rapport. There are lots of people around to talk to for a brief time but no one who is really listening to what you are saying. I have this feeling that the people I know are politely waiting for me to stop talking so that they may tell me about their problems. I suppose I expect too much from people when I want them to care about me as a person. In this day and age, everything is very impersonal and no one wants to be involved in someone else's life. If you let down the barriers, you become dependent, and no one wants that. Most of all I miss being able to tell someone what I feel and have someone tell me that it will work out regardless of what happens.

I wish I had the nerve to send in the card for computer dating, but I am afraid they would send me some character that I would hate the sight of and whom I would never be able to get rid of without becoming violent. I guess I will put the telephone number away and wait until I am a little more desperate. That could be tomorrow!

Love,
Adrianne

December 8, 1973

Dear Andrew,

Happy December! You really have become a mean son of a bitch. This new personality of yours is very difficult for me to become accustomed to. I keep thinking of you as a rational human being with whom I should be able to hold a rational conversation. When you start swearing and shouting over something you don't understand, I react by hanging up. This slows down the wheels of communication. Then I always have to call my lawyer. Then she calls your lawyer. Then your lawyer calls you. Finally you call back and halfway apologize for having behaved like a dumb ass.

This has happened several times, and I keep thinking that you will catch on and save time for all of us. I have no intention of cheating you in any way. I do expect you to live up to the letter of the divorce agreement. Anytime you don't, I will let you know and I will reinforce the facts by calling my lawyer. I should think you could understand this but it is the same game each time there is a conflict.

It is your responsibility to pay for the books that the children use in college. I will make sure that you receive an itemized list so that there is no doubt about what you have to pay. What I don't understand is why you didn't ask for the list instead of throwing a telephone temper tantrum in terms of the fact that you were not paying for any more books for the children. I know I am nuts since the divorce, but when I talk to you I feel almost sane and rational. One thing certain, Christmastime is the season of goodness and brotherhood but it has not influenced you in any way. I am afraid that after our conversation I find myself hoping that all the needles drop off your Christmas tree. And then, you may guess what I think you should do with the trunk of that same Christmas tree.

Cussedly,
Adrianne

December 20, 1973

Happy Jingle-bells, Andrew,

Everyone is filled with the joy of the holidays. Snow has touched the world, and Merry Christmas is on everyone's lips. I passed the counter of mistletoe and suddenly realized that I would never again be kissed by you or probably by any other man. It is frightening to think about spending the next forty years without ever being hugged or kissed by a man who says he loves you. All of a sudden I can't remember what it was like to be in the circle of your arms. When I close my eyes, your face no longer appears. I can't remember what it was like to have your lips on mine. I only know there is an emptiness within me that never stops. How horrible to think of forty years stretching ahead of me without anyone to share it. Is it possible that I will endure without a kiss or a caress? I don't want this to happen, but how do you reach out and become a part of someone's life? Would I ever want to take the chance of being hurt again? Would I ever be able to believe in love? Christmas is a time of love. Maybe love will find me.

Hopefully,
Adrianne

December 30, 1973

Dear Andrew,

You have done it now. I have never heard such a string of abusive words since my grandmother used to swear at me. This time it was our son. Change that! It was my son. I got the distinct impression that you were no longer to be referred to as Scott's father. Why did you let this happen?

Wasn't it sad enough that your daughter refuses to see you? How could you completely alienate Scott?

Somehow I think it is more than bitterness on the part of the children. You are doing something wrong. Scott went on seeing you, he met your wife and her two children, and in his way he tried to keep the lines of communication open between the two of you. Why did you have to make him feel so unwanted? I don't understand how it is possible for you to allow your own children to turn away from you.

Before the divorce I thought it was strange when you told me you did not want the children. I didn't believe you, but now I do. You don't want to face the complications that come with teenagers. Dealing with their personalities is beyond your capability. I know that Scott was often rude when he came over, but were you the perfect host? Couldn't you see that he walked into a situation that used to be his home and his father? Scott is not the type to be impressed when you showed him your latest tape player and tapes when he knew the money came from cuttting his expenses for college. When you showed off your new family's recently purchased possessions with such pride, you made it more painful for Scott to accept what he had lost. Maybe he didn't lose that much. If you are that insensitive to the emotional needs of your children, they may be better off without you. I wonder if you are capable of loving anyone but yourself?

Sometimes I have this horrible feeling that you never loved me. I think I was someone to write your college papers, solve your problems, care for the children, keep the budget, and work around the house. As long as I was a convenience, you stayed around. When I got excited about my own teaching, it was less convenient for you so you traded me in for a traditional doormat-type wife who accepted your bi-sexual tendencies. All along it was for your well-being. I kept thinking you would still try to be a father but that meant caring about your children. Evidently that is too much to expect from you.

I am sad that Scott will not be able to count on you. I am still dumb enough to think that Leslie and Scott both need a father. Now I have to face the fact that you have not been a father for a very long time. It may be easier to face the future without knowing the children are hurt by seeing you. My hurt continues whether I see you or not.

When I see the children so angry and hurt, I have this recurring fantasy: I keep meeting you at Air-Mart. Your current wife, her children, and the superintendent of the Middletown schools are standing there in the main aisle talking. I am wearing the old pointed-toed shoes. I simply walk over and I kick you as hard as I can in the balls. Everyone is horrified! You are in great agony. Before I turn and walk away, I manage to smile and say: "I owed you that. I think you should stay out of Air-Mart for a while."

Love,
Adrianne

P.S. A belated Merry Christmas, faggot! I hope with the cold weather that yours falls off!

January 3, 1974

Dear Andrew,

To avoid the swearing confrontations that phone calls create, I now send you letters to vehemently remind you when the college book money for the children is due. You must have masochistic tendencies. No one would be interested in reading the unkind letters that I actually mail to you. Why don't you simply send the book money unless I notify you that the children are no longer enrolled in college? Why do you have to have a sarcastic, insulting letter from me before you send the money?

It must be Freudian! You are feeling guilty, and my letters are a form of punishment that you think you deserve. Well, whatever turns you on. If you want letters before you will send the book money, believe me you will get letters.

The best part for me is picking out some very feminine paper and envelopes. I like the pale lavender. Then I make sure that I put my name in the corner where the return address goes. Then I sprinkle the envelope with strong perfume. It must give your second wife quite a thrill when it arrives. I wonder if you share the letters of abuse with her or do you make her jealous? Maybe you both have mental quirks. I know I do.

Love,
Adrianne

January 9, 1974

Dear Andrew,

This is the coldest, bleakest day I have ever experienced. There wasn't any snow, only dark gloomy hours that seemed to last for an eternity. For being the last day of Christmas vacation it was a real bad siege. Leslie had made plans to be with Mark. I was completely at loose ends. Leslie and I had put the Christmas mess away and cleaned the house. All of my papers were graded and I had planned what I would be teaching when I went back to school. Everyone I called was gone for the day.

The television was one soap opera after another. Everybody all over the networks was getting divorced. The radio was news or rock music. None of these had any soothing effect on my ragged nerves. I haven't had such a miserable day in a long time. I found myself wishing that there was a switch on my body that would turn me off until morning. I tried to take a nap but I was not sleepy. I am ashamed to admit that I still have these hopeless days, but I guess they are a part of divorce. Certainly with school starting tomorrow, it has to be better.

Sadly,
Adrianne

Dear Andrew,

I love my son! I love my son! I love my son! I keep telling myself that I do love my son. I don't like him, but I love him. The reason I don't like him is because I find it impossible to like a pack rat. I try to accept the fact that he loves antiques. I try to accept the fact that he is reluctant to part with anything. I almost succeed until I try to walk through my house. My house has become his private warehouse. Scott sneaks things in when I am at school.

The front porch is enclosed, and for a long time he has had odd pieces of furniture and boxes of books stored out there. That didn't bother me greatly because I am able to make it from the front door to the inside of the living room with my eyes shut. I don't have to look at the porch. I choose to believe that the front porch no longer exists.

The four rocking chairs, the bolts of velvet upholstery material, the boxes of records, books, and odd pieces of china that are stored in his bedroom scarcely bother me. I keep the door shut and pretend that the room was stolen by gypsies. Today when I got home, I made the mistake of walking into the dining room. Since my kitchen is too small for a table, I find myself eating a meal on rare occasions in the dining room. This is no longer possible. The table was covered with patterned glass, the seat to the van was on the end in the corner, there were boxes stacked in every open space, and there were a couple of odd chairs. I am sure that these things belong to Scott. I am sure there is a logical reason why all these things are in my dining room, but at this point he has not left a note nor sent a phone message saying that he would return.

I may simply advertise a rummage sale and sell everything that isn't nailed down. I bet that would shake him up. Sometimes I wonder about him. I wonder if it occurred to him that I might have had a guest for the evening meal. Actually he knows that I never have company. Christmas, Thanksgiving, and birthdays are when I cook and serve a

144

meal in the dining room, so he was pretty safe. I hope these items are here on a temporary basis. I have this horrible feeling that I am living in the middle of an antique warehouse. Would you like to store your body here with the other ruins?

Love,
Adrianne

January 23, 1974

Dear Andrew,

For some reason I am always becoming involved in the strangest situations. About a month ago one of the secretaries at the superintendent's office asked me if I would be interested in talking about antiques to a group to which her mother belonged. I told Becky that I knew very little about antiques. The antiques were my son's specialty. Becky, however, had heard me talking to the parent group that worked with our school band and she thought I would be an interesting speaker because I have a humorous outlook on life. I told her that I would be willing to talk about collector's items or things that might be thrown away in spring cleaning without realizing that the item might have value to a collector. She said she would have her mother call me.

Becky's mother called that evening and I agreed to talk about items that some people collect and other people throw away. After I agreed I discovered I would be speaking to one of the historical societies from a neighboring county. Nothing like jumping in over my head. I got together about fifty items that would qualify as collectibles and found out something interesting that pertained to them. I packed all the items in a large suitcase and hoped I would remember what I was supposed to say about the various items.

I got to the historical society early so I had time to set things up for my speech. I had it arranged so that I gave an introduction and a few definitions. The rest of the speech was concerned with taking items out of the suitcase, unwrapping them, and telling about them. Then I passed out the items into the audience so they could see them first-hand. It was an older group of men and women, and they seemed genuinely interested in what I had to say.

For some reason I had forgotten how much I enjoyed talking to a group of people. I like to watch their reactions to see if I am able to make them smile or laugh or understand my point. I suppose every teacher is a frustrated actress. Half of the fun of teaching is the reaction of the students to your comments.

I was pleased when the members of the historical society seemed to enjoy my presentation. After I had finished, many of them stayed to ask questions—fortunately, questions I was able to answer. It gave me a good feeling to know that I was doing something that gave people pleasure; it was a nice way to spend a Sunday afternoon.

Talking to a group brought back many pleasant memories. When I was in college I belonged to a speaker's bureau. I spoke to clubs and various organizations almost on the basis of one a week. In college it kept me busy and once in awhile I made a little money. I would like to get back on the speaking circuit but I am not sure how I would start. Maybe someone else will call. Could you use a lecture on nouns and verbs at your school? I could rush right over.

Love,
Adrianne

February 5, 1974

Dear Andrew,

Tonight I have decided to face some facts. It has been two years since the divorce. Obviously, I am not going to die from a broken heart. It is equally obvious that I am never going to commit suicide. This basically rules out the fact that I am going to die. If I am not going to die, I must be going to live. If I am going to live, I have to do a better job of it than what I have. If the past two years have been living, then forget it; I have to face the fact that I need to get out and to meet people and to become a part of the world. This sounds great but I don't know how to put it into practice.

As a teacher, there is no opportunity to meet eligible men. The men teachers are married and for the most part so are most of the parents. No one on the faculty knows anyone in my age bracket, so I can't count on an introduction from my colleagues. There is no point in sitting in a bar drinking a Coke. The men I might meet would not be ones I'd be interested in knowing. So far there aren't many men falling all over themselves at the Mall or the grocery store in order to meet me. Church isn't the answer because I believe in God, not churches.

There should be a logical way to meet someone but so far my best idea comes in the form of putting an ad in the local paper. I can see it now: "English teacher is interested in companion who would like to help her grade papers." In all the books I have read or movies that I have seen, there are supposed to be two or three fantastically rich and devastatingly charming men fighting over me. There is a wide gap between fiction and real life.

I won't say that I am desperate for male companionship but when I read about the recent series of rapes at the local Mall, I decided that might resolve part of my problem. I invested in a sweatshirt with big letters that proclaimed: "RAPE HERE!" I spent several long afternoons and evenings strolling up and down the length of the Mall and through the parking lot but nothing happened. That was a little obvious! It was, however, the best idea that I have had to date.

My second idea was to carry a sign that said: "Date me, I give green stamps." Apparently there aren't too many men in this area who are interested in filling their green stamp books. I didn't get any takers. They say it pays to advertise but maybe I am not being subtle enough.

I put a bear trap next to the electric meter outside the house, but I had to throw the meter reader back because he was too young and too married. The same thing happened with the postman. The world is full of twenty-five-year-old married men. Even their fathers are married. You see, I am checking every angle.

Here I am writing comedy lines, and I am crying. Where does a forty-year-old woman go to meet a man? I'm sure there is an answer, but right now I can't find it. I should call you up and see if you are interested in fooling around with an attractive, dark-haired divorcee. That would be irony of the first degree.

Hopelessly,
Adrianne

February 7, 1974

Dear Andrew,

I do find myself in some interesting situations. The weather was bad. Mark had spent the night because the roads were so slippery. About half an hour after he started home this morning, he was back, knocking on the front door. Big Red, which is what he calls his 1942 converted fire truck, had stopped on the highway going home. He hitchhiked back for help. So that meant that Leslie and I took the 1969 Falcon and started back with him.

Somehow the thought of my little Falcon pulling his enormous truck was dismaying. But Leslie and I have learned to handle these situations as they occur. We slipped and slid out to the highway. Mark hooked a long rope from the Falcon to the truck. Leslie is a better driver in snow and ice than I am so she was at the wheel of the Falcon. I sat in the front seat with her and crossed my fingers and prayed. I had visions of the truck sliding into the back and crushing us.

Fortunately, it is a game little Falcon because with a little straining and pulling it took off pulling Big Red down the road. Before long Mark signaled that Big Red had started. We stopped and he undid the rope. We followed him home to make sure that he got there safely, and then we came back home. It was funny, while we were in the process of pulling Big Red, one of my students drove past and waved. I bet he wondered what in the heck I was doing trying to pull an enormous truck with my little old car. It just goes to show that positive thinking sometimes works.

I think I need to concentrate all my thoughts on getting rid of my low spirits. I know it has to come from me but it is difficult.

February 12, 1974

Dear Andrew,

My first date was this evening. If this is the standard date for a divorce, it may well be my last date. One of the younger teachers at school knew that I was lonesome so she offered to invite me over for a spaghetti supper so that I could meet her father. Her father had been divorced for a number of years. Tari Weber explained that he drank a great deal but I figured a warm drunk body was better than no body at all. I was very wrong!

I put on my best bib and tucker and arrived on time. He looked a great deal like Sergeant Carter from the old Gomer Pyle television show. My date for the evening was a retired army man, and in this day and age of longer hair, he still wore a regulation crew cut. I resisted the temptation to salute. He was very polite. We had a polite conversation while we waited for supper. He seemed to have a little difficulty focusing. I had the feeling that he kept seeing two of me. One of him was quite enough. He was a nice person but he was very full of alcohol. He managed

149

to get out to the table. The spaghetti was delicious but since I didn't drink, he made up for the both of us. Tari had long ago reached the stage of not being embarrassed for him. She had told me he drank so I knew exactly what I was getting into. The question was how to get out of it.

The meal was a semi-disaster because spaghetti is not the meal for a man who has been drinking to try and eat. We were all a little uncomfortable but we talked around it. Later we watched a little television and then I made an excuse to leave. A little polite conversation goes a long way.

It was touchingly sad when he rose to shake hands and wound up kissing my hand. We both knew it was a first and a last meeting. Another time and another place it might have been different, but as it was, he was an alcoholic and I was a proper English teacher. That made us worlds apart. It will be an evening I won't forget because I will always wonder why a basically nice person has to drink himself into oblivion. Is this what happens when you are alone and divorced too long? I hope not. It seems like such a waste. When he asked how long I had been divorced and I said two years, he made an interesting comment. He said, "You poor soul, that's like a new amputation." He was right. It is still new, and it still hurts. I wonder if I will ever get over the pain and the loneliness. Will I ever stop feeling like half a person?

It was not a successful evening in many ways, yet I am grateful that one person cared enough to try to help me. It does restore my faith in people. I also know that I am learning from every experience. In some ways I am learning more from the experiences that are unsuccessful. They do make me more content with my single lot. Not a whole lot more, but they help. Oh, Andrew, I still miss you deeply.

Love,
Adrianne

February 18, 1974

Dear Andrew,

There is nothing illegal, subversive, or un-American about Scott calling your school office and leaving messages. As I look at it, he is being rather tactful for Scott. I could think of several more colorful words that he might have been tempted to use. The fact that he tells the secretary that he is Scott Helman and that he wants her to tell you that your only true and legitimate son is alive and well doesn't seem so terrible to me. I think he has a right to communicate with you and to let you know how he feels about the situation. No, I can't share your sentiments that it is a filthy Communist plot to discredit you as a principal.

Somehow I believe I would rather have messages from Scott than the total silence you receive from Leslie. Now I admit that neither one is a healthy relationship between a father and his two children, but there is little that I may do. I have maintained from the beginning that you love them and that they have a right and a responsibility to see you. I explained to them that I would manage even if they met your new wife and family. I have this stupid feeling that regardless of the divorce the children have a right to some of your time, attention, and love as a father. If you remember, I made certain financial concessions to insure this right. I have never tried to keep them from having a loving and working relationship with you. I don't honestly think that you can say you have tried to foster any type of fatherly understanding. I like to think you do not want to see them because you are afraid you might corrupt them. I am afraid your attitude is not that noble. I am afraid you don't want to be bothered with them or their problems.

You and Scott will have to work out your problem. I think he loves you and misses you and wants attention from you. At the same time, he is hurt and disappointed and wants vengeance. Until you two are able to talk to each other this situation will probably continue. I know that if I asked Scott to stop calling you, he would. I don't feel that

151

I have the right to do this. He is communicating with you the only way that he knows how. Communicate back to him. Make your decision. If you love your son and want to be his father, then let him know that he is important to you. If he is simply an irritating complication in your busy new life, tell him. In other words, don't call me. Get off the fence and let him know where he stands in your life.

Please refrain from calling to tell me that you are going to have my son arrested for harassing you by phone. I am afraid that if you told the police the message was: "Tell my father that his only son is alive and well," they would lock you up. If you consider Scott's words a threat, you have a guilt complex deeper than I am capable of helping or understanding. You may not be as happy as you profess. You have my sympathy.

Love,
Adrianne

February 26, 1974

Dear Andrew,

Scott came home for a short visit. His visits are quite predictable. Whenever he is low on funds he manages to appear close to a mealtime. In one visit he is able to do his laundry, inhale all the food in sight, and place several long-distance calls to far-off places. I have mixed emotions when I see him drive up to the house. I should have a sign put on the door that says I will meet him at the laundromat or the nearest restaurant. Surely it would be cheaper than having the triple threat enter the house.

You miss a great deal by not having him drop in to visit with you. I am sure that he would be glad to raid your food supply, exhaust your laundry facilities, and run up your phone bill. Only a little bit of encouragement from you could give him a father and you all these fatherly pleasures. It is sad that you do not communicate with him. I may joke about what happens when he visits but at the

same time I am always glad to see him. In my own way
I am proud of him. Scott is striving to find his place in a
complex modern world. I don't always agree with or even
approve of his tactics but I admire his spirit. He is man-
aging to hang in there and cope with the world of adulthood.

One of these days, he may even be a successful antique
dealer. He is very young, and he has learned a great deal.
Of course, he still has a great deal more to learn, but we
all do. Learning is a big chunk of living. I think when we
stop learning, we stop living. With time and experience, he
has an interesting future. He may never be rich but he is
pleased with his way of life and that is very important.
At times, I still envy him. If I ever loosen up and decide
on a direction, I too may find the bluebird of happiness
after all. Then again I may find it in time to watch it poop
on my head. You never really know about bluebirds, or
happiness, or poop!

Love,
Adrianne

March 1, 1974

Dear Andrew,

All the losers of the world must have gotten together
this evening as members of the Singles Club. The ad in the
paper suggested that if you were single, divorced, or
widowed and between the ages of 21 and 45, you might
find fun and friendship as a member of the newly formed
Singles Club of Middletown, Indiana. Since it was meeting
at a local church, I figured that it couldn't be all bad.

I arrived promptly at seven-thirty, breaking the first
rule. No one is the first to arrive at a Singles Club. It makes
you look eager. The second person to arrive was the acting
president. He was a local insurance agent at least ten years
younger than I was. He made meaningful comments as he
bustled around fixing the coffee. The next ten people to
come in were short, fat, tall, or thin variations of husband-

hunting females. That was the first time I have ever seen one man engulfed in a band of ten women. The second rule must be to get in there and get a toehold because the women outnumber the men. The next man to come in weighed every bit of four hundred pounds. I have seen big people before, but he was fantastic. I was nearer his age, and it frightened me the way he kept looking at my breasts. Whatever message he was sending, I was not receiving.

Taking inventory, we had something like six females for every male. Most of the males were pushing to reach twenty-five. They were dishwashers, certified public accountants, shoe salesmen, assistant produce managers for local groceries, insurance salesmen, or unemployed. The women were nurses, teachers, check-out clerks, unemployed, or most unbearable of all—waitresses. From the random comments, most of the men had been divorced at least once and were making enormous support payments. Most of the women were divorced either twice or they had never been married. The men were either grossly underweight or overweight. The average height must have been five feet one. The women were mostly tall. Several of them were overweight. One of them was completely deaf. One of the men was in braces up to his hips. Everyone stood out because of some peculiarity. Maybe I was overly sensitive but even putting myself in with the group, I could only come out saying we were a bunch of losers. Let's face it, being with a group of people in worse shape than I was, was not the answer to my problem. I lasted through the meeting, which was a business meeting to elect officers and plan an agenda. Somehow building a float to represent the Singles Club in the Historical Parade, playing coeducational volleyball at the local YMCA, or sharing a carry-in dinner at the reservoir was not what I had in mind. This did not seem to be an answer to boredom.

I don't know what I had in mind, but I know the Singles Club was not the answer. I know I am overweight. I know I am lonely. I know I have problems. I know these things, and I can face them. I can't face being in a group that would reinforce these things. I tried to get out in a hurry but I had to pass the four hundred pounds of eye contact. With a brief glance at my face, he zeroed in on a full stare at my left breast while he said he hoped he'd see us at the next meeting. If my breasts are interested and want to go by themselves, they have my permission. As for me, I'll take a rerun on television or maybe a quick cut across the wrists with a sharp razor blade. A quick death would have to be an improvement.

Love,
Adrianne

March 6, 1974

Dear Andrew,

Whenever I receive a phone call at school, it always frightens me until I find out what it is about. This afternoon I was more frightened when I got the message. It was from Scott, and he was at Williamsburg, Indiana. He and his partner had packed the can and started toward Hamilton, Ohio, to do a big antique show. They got as far as Williamsburg and the van gave out. The filling station was small and totally unequipped to cope with a Volks van that dates back a hundred years.

Scott wanted to know if I could pick up a U-Rent and meet them in Williamsburg and then take them on to Hamilton, Ohio. It was not exactly what I had in mind for the evening, but since the divorce my motto has become: "Something to do is better than nothing to do." Before this was over, I would have been glad to settle for nothing.

School was almost over for the afternoon but I had to call and cancel my appointment at the beauty salon. That meant my hair would look terrible, but it was a small scrifice to make for the promising future of Indiana's youngest antique dealer. I left school as soon as it was possible and headed for the U-Rent place on Madison. They had plenty of the trailers sitting on the lot but they couldn't put them on the road because they were out of contracts.

So I drove down to the next place. They were getting ready to hitch it up as I started to write the check. Then the attendant informed me that he didn't take checks. I can hardly wait for the bank to tell me again that a check is better than money. Nothing is better than money when you have problems. I told the filling station attendant to hold everything and I would be right back. Then I drove to the bank, cashed a check, and drove back. This time they hooked it up and glady accepted my cold cash.

Driving in a normal situation and being afraid is nothing compared with the fear of driving while you have an enormous empty U-Rent on the back of a very small Falcon. I decided not to worry but to keep going and pray that I would be able to find Scott and his partner at the right filling station. After an eternity, I finally saw the van. March is not the warmest month in the year and before we got all the stuff in the U-Haul, I thought we were going to freeze.

The people at the local filling sation were very nice. They said the boys could leave the van until it would be convenient to pick it up. It is refreshing to know that there are still some kind people in the world. The best thing that could happen now would be for someone to steal the van. That kind of luck I don't have.

Scott took over the driving, and I was glad; my nerves are a little slow in warming up to these traumatic situations. It seemed like it took forever to get to Hamilton, Ohio. It must have been at least nine o'clock. I was afraid the hall where they were having the show would be locked, but I guess they are used to dealers coming in at odd hours hours. I felt sorry for the boys. Their booth was on the second floor and that meant that everything in the U-Rent had to be carried up two flights of stairs.

It took about two hours to get everything unloaded. Then we unhooked the U-Rent and parked it. The boys would have to set up the antiques in a beautiful display.

All I had to do was find my way back to Middletown, Indiana. I hoped I could do it without getting lost. I told the boys that I would be back before the show was over on Sunday to get them back to Middletown.

Late hours are not for me. I was sleepy and the best was yet to come. Fog started drifting in, and I could hardly see the road in front of me. I would have been terrified but I was too frightened. I kept hoping that I wouldn't get lost. Fortunately on a night like that there was very little traffic.

At three this morning I got back into the safety of my house. I decided to try for a couple of hours of sleep before time to get ready for school. I didn't look forward to teaching but I was pleased that some way, somehow, I had lived through another impossible situation. I frantically prayed that the boys would have a good show. I hated to think what would happen if they didn't.

Oh, Andrew, you are missing some rare experiences. Your life surely can't hold a candle to this.

Love,
Adrianne

March 10, 1974

Dear Andrew,

The boys had a good show in Hamilton. Life keeps throwing in a little good news to keep us going. I drove over this afternoon and found the place with only a minimum of trouble. I turned the wrong way on a one-way street but no one seemed to notice. After parking near the U-Rent, I went in to the show and spent some time looking at antiques. I like to look at them. I am always fascinated by the historical significance and the price tag. If I were rich, I think I could become a collector. I don't suppose I will ever have that problem.

When the show ended at six, the boys started packing up all the glass and china. After everything was packed in boxes, we had to wait to get in a parking place near the door so we would not have to carry the furniture and boxes a mile to the U-Rent. It was a little tricky getting all the wires and everything hooked back up for the tail lights on the U-Rent, but Scott and I are both getting pretty good at wiring things in the dark. Scott and Jeff finally got everything loaded and we started back to Middletown. Once again we were lucky—the fog rolled in right on schedule. This time it was worse because we had the massive U-Rent following us.

Scott and I are both super cautious so we drove slowly and steadily while Jeff slept. I wish I could be as unconcerned about everything as Jeff is. When he has nothing else to do, he nods off. I suppose it must be a restful and healthy way of living. I strained my eyes and helped Scott watch for road signs, the edge of the road, and low-flying airplanes.

We eventually got back to Middletown. They unloaded the U-Rent, and when that was finished, Scott and I took the U-Rent back to the filling station. No one was there but they had told us to unhook it and push it back into place. That's what we did. Then I dropped Scott off and came back into place. It had been a very, very long day. Once again it was a few brief hours of sleep before I would go into the world of education.

I can't help but feel like you are missing some fantastic experiences.

Love,
Adrianne

P.S. I told Scott we would rest on Monday, and on Tuesday we would pick up a tow bar and go after the broken van. That should be another fun trip. Want to join us?

Dear Andrew,

I left school with the school buses and picked Scott and Jeff up at the shop. Then we drove over to a rent-everything place and had a tow bar put on the back of the Falcon. Then we started back for Williamsburg and the ailing van. It was still there. No one had the decency to either steal it or put it completely out of its misery.

After some backing up and going forward and pushing, pulling, and straining, the boys got the van hitched to the tow bar. There was still one major problem, you can't turn those things around on a dime, and we were headed in the opposite direction from Middletown. The only thing we could do was keep driving until we found a road to turn off on. In the country finding a block to go around is a little different than doing the same thing in the city. In the country, you are taking the tour of round-robin's barn. This could be miles of bumpy road.

We finally found a road and turned down it. It was a washboard. We could only drive about five miles an hour for fear the van would bounce off the back. I died a thousand deaths. I knew that van would be in my back seat before we ever got pointed in the direction of Middletown. After what seemed an eternity we finally managed to get back to the highway. Then we drove slowly back to Middletown. I prayed we would get there before we got caught in the dark and the fog.

Once we hit Middletown, we had to drive the length of it to get it to a place where someone operated on Volkswagen buses. After we got the monster unhitched, we went uptown and got something to eat. It is not easy being the mother of a son who can only be described as an accident looking for a place to happen. That type of son makes motherhood more difficult.

There are times, my love, when I would gladly give you custody of your son and all his imaginative and innovative problems. One thing I can say is that Scott constantly gives me a variety of problems. I never have to worry about experiencing the same old ones over and over. I miss your stability at times like this.

Love,
Adrianne

P.S. If you could stabilize your sex preference we could talk.

March 23, 1974

Dear Andrew,

The world is filled with lonely people trying to make contact with each other. There was an article in the newspaper that advertised a lecture at Mason State College on Extra Sensory Perception. Since I teach a class called: Witches, Warlocks, and Other Weirdos that deals with the occult, the supernatural, and psychic phenomena, I thought it might be worth a dollar and fifty cents to attend.

The lecture was interesting, and I did get some material that I could use in class. The lecture itself was a gigantic sales pitch for a series of lectures, books, pamphlets, special readings, and so forth that were all connected with something called the Inner Soul Movement. If you liked the first lecture you were encouraged to spend three dollars and attend a four-hour workshop the following evening.

Being the game soul that I am, I attended. It was interesting to note that most of the people who had attended were divorced, widowed, single, or separated. For them it was a way of meeting people who shared an interest in the area of psychic phenomena. I had stumbled into this accidentally. Those people were so lonely and so eager to talk to another person that they were willing to pay one hundred and twenty-five dollars to sign up for the whole course so they would have some place to go and people whom they could communicate with.

For a little while I was tempted to sign up and become

part of something. Then I realized that for me buying time with people was not the answer to being alone. It might work for some people but I knew it was too commercial an answer for me. Whatever takes me out of this feeling of loneliness will have to be a natural situation.

Sometimes I think we live in a cold and non-caring world when people have to pay to meet each other. Where are the friends, neighbors, and relatives who should be working to bring lonely people together? In some way I am becoming accustomed to my loneliness. I don't like it but I am not so afraid of it as I once was.

Love,
Adrianne

April 8, 1974

Dear Andrew,

Scott and Jeff were doing an antique show in Greenville, Indiana. That is about fifty-five miles from here. Leslie and Mark had done their good deed by helping to take the stuff over in Big Red. Going over was not a bad situation; they got there without any problems. Sunday, in order to speed things up, Leslie, Mark, and I went over to help. We got things packed up in record time. With all of us working, we had that truck loaded very promptly. We had a tarp over the back to hold the boxes and furniture in place.

On the way back Leslie and Mark rode in Big Red. Scott, Jeff, and I rode in the Opel following the truck. It was dark and traffic was moving along pretty well. Then I noticed that the tarp had pulled loose and things were beginning to fly out the back of Big Red. Scott started honking and honking and flashing his lights. Big Red just kept chugging along. Finally the oncoming traffic eased and Scott started around Big Red. Scott drives like a madman, and I am always frightened. With him darting around the side of the truck I was petrified. We finally got Mark's attention and he pulled off along the side of the road.

One of the fasteners on the tarp had pulled off so we

were at a loss as to what to do. Only a few pieces of paper had blown out, but the other things were getting a little jumbled. The only way that we could think of to hold the tarp down was for someone to sit on top of it. The choices were limited. Mark was the only one who could drive Big Red. Leslie would have to ride with Mark, or they would never volunteer the truck again. I couldn't drive the Opel because it was a stick shift. Jeff shouldn't drive because he had night blindness. That meant Scott would have to drive the Opel. Jeff and I lost. We were elected to ride in the back of the truck on top of the tarp.

Again I proved that being divorced is a form of growing insanity. Jeff and I hauled our bodies up into the back of the truck and spread our bodies over the tarp to hold it down in as many places as possible. We started off. I couldn't believe it. The wind was so strong that it nearly flipped us off the tarp. For once I was glad that I was on the fat side. Otherwise I might have blown off into the countryside. As it was, it was nerve-racking to keep the tarp held in place. We were sitting on splintery boards and moving canvas. It was quite an experience. Jeff entertained me by telling long stories about his strange relatives.

Things were going quite well until the tailgate in the center of Big Red broke loose and flew off, narrowly missing the front of the Opel. Thank God, Scott had not been tailgating! The gate went bouncing off the road with sparks flying from the metal as it struck. The Opel slammed on the brakes and then recovered. Scott started honking and Jeff and I started hollering. Leslie and Mark ignored everything. Once again the little Opel went tearing around the side and waved Mark off the road. Then Scott went back after the tailgate and I caught my breath and said my prayers. If that tailgate had landed on the front of the Opel, it could have been a terrible wreck.

Scott brought the tailgate back, and we put it on the floor of the truck. We did not want to risk having it fly off into space again. Now all Jeff and I had to worry about was keeping ourselves from flying out the back of Big Red. I think it was the longest ride I ever had. By the time we got back and got unloaded my hair was standing on end. I felt like I had sailed the seven seas the hard way. I don't really get scared until after these things are over, and then I spend a lot of time quietly shaking. What will happen next?

Love,
Adrianne

April 15, 1974

Dear Andrew,

Cash is no longer king. This is the era of the credit card. I have fought it as long as I could but I realize now that a person without a credit card is a person without an identity. Someone has told me that it was difficult for a divorced woman to obtain credit. I thought this was stretching the truth. Little did I know what it meant to try to obtain a credit account with Sears.

Leslie and I went in on a Saturday and decided to purchase a rug for the living room. The holes in the one we had were so large we kept tripping through them. When we went into Sears, I had enough money in my checking account to pay for a rug. I decided that this would be a good time to open a credit account. I had not used any form of credit since the divorce. If I couldn't pay for it, I did not buy it. This was a terrible mistake on my part. I did not anticipate a problem with Sears because you and I had always had an account with them while we were married. Something seems to happen to the credit for the woman. I filled out all the forms and answered all the questions about my life and financial situation. They told me to call Monday afternoon to see if my credit was approved. Apparently they could not handle this on Saturday.

Monday I called and my credit had not been established. I was told by the unfriendliest voice in the world to call back on the following day. Tuesday I was a little less friendly when I called. An unconcerned voice told me to call back on Wednesday. I asked if there was a problem, and they did not seem to have an answer. I called back on Wednesday and it seems there was a slight problem. Because I had not charged anything I did not have a credit rating. Without a credit rating, I could not charge anything. The voice of Sears seemed to think that by Thursday they would have the credit situation worked out to their satisfaction. I have a lot of patience but it was wearing thin. Thursday morning I called and they did not know anything. At that point, I got tired of being polite and patient so I asked to speak to the credit manager of Sears. He was too busy to talk to me. So then I asked the name of the person to whom I was speaking. It was a Miss Brewster.

So I said something to the effect that Miss Brewster should listen carefully. I told her that at this point I did not care whether I bought the rug there or not. I explained that I owned two houses, two cars, two children, two registered dachshunds, two savings accounts and that I had a tenure job as a schoolteacher and I did not owe any bills to anybody. Then I told Miss Brewster that Sears could either establish my credit or cancel the order because I would go somewhere else and write a check to purchase a rug. I did not need their credit or their rug. I used my most determined tone of voice. She said she would relay the message and I could call back. That did it. I unleashed my temper and told her there was no way I would call her back. When she had cleared my credit she could either call me or forget it. Then I hung up.

Fifteen minutes later the phone rang. A charming male voice said: "Mrs. Helman, this is Sears Department Store. When would you like for us to deliver your rug?" Magically, they were able to establish my credit without any further problem. A smile and a winning way are sometimes a big fat waste of time. Now at least I have my own personal account at Sears. What a triumph!

Love,
Adrianne

April 23, 1974

Dear former husband,

    Auctions are getting me into some interesting situations. Today I attended an exclusive auction at the Wooded Hills Country Club of Raymont, Indiana. Clinton, my favorite auctioneer, had a special estate auction of exclusive glass and china. It was a little unusual to have an auction at a private country club so I was looking forward to attending. Clinton was charging a three-dollar entry fee to be able to bid. The fee included a buffet, so it was a refreshing change from a country auction where you stand in manure all day. Life goes from one extreme to another.

    This auction was pure luxury. I decided to dress for the occasion. I put on one of my better-looking dresses and made myself look like the darling of the society pages. Then I added enough diamond rings to look more than a little ostentatious. I figured that I might as well look the part of the mad, carefree, eccentric divorcee who was having an afternoon of frivolity at the country club auction. It was not a part that I had played before, but it seemed like a fun way to go. My English and drama background are coming through to help me survive the days alone. Before I go somewhere I pretend I am acting the part of a certain type of person. This amuses me and takes my mind off of being alone. Today's role should be quite amusing because I doubt if there would be anyone there who would connect me with the drab English teacher of country auctions.

    The auction was interesting because most of the people who were there were people who were bored. It was written all over their faces. They wanted to be amused by the novelty of the auction. The regular dealers for a Clinton auction would not pay three dollars to go to an auction so they were not there. That meant that without the regular dealers to keep the prices steady it was a strange auction. If two people were amused by the same item, the bidding went ridiculously high. It was a rich person's game, and I found it amusing. By the same token, some of the nicest pieces of glass slipped through at low prices because they did not particularly strike anyone's fancy. That was what I had expected. As a result I had a fun afternoon, looked impressive, and picked up a few good items for the shop.

No one swept me off my feet in a romantic manner or asked me to run off to Las Vegas for a fling, but I did have a nice afternoon. I told myself that since no one knew who I was except the auctioneer, that I had probably set a few hearts on fire. I am sure that at least one of the men went away thinking: "Why didn't I try to meet the lovely, mysterious lady?" Well, let's face it. Whoever he was, he blew it! I doubt if I'll ever pass his way again. I am sure he will never be in my English class. I wonder how many romances did not blossom because I was aloof and he was slow. Dream on, I keep telling myself! Dream on! There has to be some kind of excitement in the future.

Woman does not live by dreams alone.

Lovingly,
Adrianne

May 1, 1974

Dear Andrew,

Doris called to tell me that Susan was walking on air. It seems that Barry realized that Susan was the one and and only girl for him. He was not only back to Middletown but he was going to transfer back to Mason State College. Then he would be able to see Susan more often. Barry had been away for almost a year and had done some heavy dating around. He came to the realization that Susan was what he wanted in his life.

I know that Susan will be delighted. She had tried to date some other young men but she had known all along that Barry was the one she wanted for a lifetime partner. I am glad that it is working out for them. I thought it would. I remember the night that Susan and I shared a pizza. I had told her then that I was sure that Barry would realize she was the girl for him. He finally did.

That same evening I said you would someday want to come back and it would be too late. That still has to be proven. I think it will happen but it will take awhile. The novelty of your situation has not worn off. One of these days, I believe that you will realize that you miss the children and me. You will know that what we had to offer was real in terms of family life. I know you will want to come back. I also know that it will be too late. The man that I loved doesn't exist anymore. I don't know what my future holds but I don't believe you will be a real part of it.

Love,
Adrianne

May 10, 1974

Dear Andrew,

It is either very late for Saturday night or very early for Sunday. I am too tired to look at the clock. I'm home from the Sushawnee Junior-Senior Prom. Since I was one of the sponsors, I had to be there. I dug out the old formal, and because tomorrow is Mother's Day, Leslie and Scott had bought me a corsage that will do double duty. The members of the junior class had worked hard on the decorations for the dance. It was a typical prom with lots of crepe paper and glitter, but they were proud of their hard work and so was I.

The last prom I had attended was one that you helped me chaperon. I remember because we had as much fun as the students. We danced and enjoyed ourselves. As long as I kept busy this evening I was doing fine. Then the band played a slow song. I found myself thinking about the way it was when we were together. I must have looked nostalgic because one of our first-year teachers danced over and insisted that I finish the dance with her husband, Bob. I know Betsy meant it as a kind gesture, and I did appreciate the thought. Our faculty is very nice. Somehow dancing with someone else's husband at that particular moment was a little more than I could handle. It only made me more aware of how alone I sometimes feel.

I danced him back and made some comment about not being able to dance with him because he was getting fresh. Then I rushed off to the kitchen to pour some punch. I am sure Bob and Betsy thought I was a little crazy but it would have been worse if I had stayed and cried. Somehow a woman my age crying at a high school prom is the epitome of insanity. So I poured the punch, hitched up my composure, and made like the devil-may-care divorcee that I am trying to become. It's a great act if I don't weaken.

At the end of the evening, the teachers who had chaperoned decided on their own to give me the center-piece to take home. This, too, was meant with all kindness and was appreciated as such. How were they to know that outside of the dozen roses you sent when Scott was born, that you had always bought me carnations? I tried to tact-fully encourage someone else to take the flowers but they wanted me to have them. So now I can't sleep because the house is filled with the soft scent of carnations and more memories than I am able to discard. It's ironic the way intended kindness can sometimes be so painful for the receiver.

Pounding the keys of the typewriter helps, but not a whole lot. I almost wish I could cry and get it over with. Women are supposed to cry because crying makes them feel better. That, too, is debatable. Crying may be the release that keeps me from falling apart but I am not sure that it or anything else can make me feel better. I miss the way of life that I knew with you. I miss what we were and what we represented. It is hard to believe that I will ever find anything to replace the way we were.

Tenderly,
Adrianne

168

May 11, 1974

Dear Andrew,

Scott left to do an antique show in Michigan, so he was not here to have lunch with Leslie and me for Mother's Day. Leslie decided to make it special. She was going to take me out for lunch at a restaurant that had only recently opened. Of course, I had to loan her the money because she did not have quite enough saved. After last night I wanted to crawl off into a corner and lick my wounds but I knew that Leslie would be disappointed. So I put on a bright face to go with a bright dress and vowed to make it a bright good lunch for both of us.

We are both gaining weight again, so we had some problems finding something dressy for a Sunday lunch at a new restaurant, but we finally got ourselves together and looked fairly decent. It was a toss-up to see who got to wear the good white shoes. Usually we don't go out at the same time, so one pair of good dress shoes works for both of us. Since it was Mother's Day, I got to wear the good shoes. I decided to make it Mother's Day all the way, so I wore the corsage. I had trouble getting the orchid to stay on properly because the material in my dress was thin and smooth and the pin wanted to slip right out.

As we got to the restaurant, the hostess came up to take us to a table for two. Leslie and I were doing our imitations of the suave sophisticated mother and daughter of the storybooks. As the hostess started to say: "Follow me," my corsage jumped off the front of my dress and fell to the floor where it lay there laughing its petals off. Everyone in the restaurant saw it happen. I was magnificently cool and composed as I retrieved it. The hostess was charming. As I picked up the corsage and started to fasten it on, she said, "Follow me as soon as you get that on." I swallowed hard to keep from laughing at her nasal twanged comment. The whole situation was a bad comedy.

When Leslie and I got to our table we hid behind our menus and cracked up. That was what we get for trying to

169

pretend we were something we weren't. We finally got control of ourselves and managed to order the meal. The food was good and Leslie was sweet. She was trying her best to make it a special lunch for me. The whole thing hit me in the heart, and I wanted to cry in the middle of my salad. I knew I was very near tears. I couldn't cry and upset her so I sat there fighting with myself. I must have been making a face because she wanted to know what was wrong. Quick thinking saved the day. I told her the salad dressing hit my sensitive tooth. Leslie bought the answer and in a few minutes I got hold of myself. The rest of the meal went smoothly.

After we ate we went over to the Mall and did a little shopping. Then we came back, and she went out to Mark's house. I let down and cried. It had been building up for several days. I don't know whether I feel better or worse but at least the tears are over for a while. I wonder if happiness is always a mixture of pleasure and pain.

Love,
Adrianne

May 19, 1974

Dear Andrew,

Shortly after the divorce I lost weight and for a time looked almost trim and slim. Then a terrible thing happened. I rediscovered food. Since then I have been on a glorious eating binge. Food has become my release. I have given up kisses for kippers, hugs for hamburgers, and passion for pastrami. My sexual satisfaction has been reduced to gobbling a hero sandwich. My most intimate contact with a man comes from drinking a Dr. Pepper.

My life is so dull I get excited when I walk past the refrigerator and it turns on. Sometimes I open and shut the door to pretend I am being winked at by the light bulb. I even get a warm glow when I bake a cake and the oven gets hot.

Food is an obsession. I find myself putting whipped cream on my cereal for breakfast. Then I have a candy bar and a glass of milk to help me make it to lunchtime. After lunch I eat cookies until suppertime. Then it is popcorn and cokes until bedtime.

I tell myself that if I eat out for a meal I will eat less. I take Leslie out for supper at four and meet Scott at six. If he is hungry, and he always is, I find myself taking him out for supper. That means I have two suppers, and I love it.

I am driving out of my way to pass bakeries so I can buy cream horns, pecan rolls, and brownies. I find myself eating until I am ill. Then I eat some more. I count calories a thousand at a time. It's ridiculous but oh, the satisfaction in a banana split! The ecstasy in a piece of butterscotch pie! I could go on and on but there is a half gallon of pecan crunch ice cream in the freezer and I plan on eating it before bedtime. God, I'm not even being a gourmet—only gross.

Heavily,
Adrianne

June 1, 1974

Dear Andrew,

The old magnetic charm is still alive and functioning. Leslie and I drove up to mother's house to spend a few days. We decided with all the traffic on Port Street that we would have a yard sale. Yard sales are always fun because you get to talk to a lot of people. I was looking my normal fat self in a pair of shorts and a blouse. Suddenly, I saw a nice car pull up and a very distinguished man got out and started talking to me.

Mother and Leslie were busy as we talked. He had an accent. He said he was Hungarian. He wondered if I lived there. I told him that I was from Middletown. He said he had a son who would be going to college there next fall. Then he asked me what my husband did. I told him that I was divorced. He wanted to know if he could call me

171

sometime when he came to Middletown to visit his son. He had an executive job for Sears, he drove a nice car, he was handsome, he was charming, and I was afraid to ask if he was married. I think I knew that he was married. He was too good to be true. So when faced with a possibility, I run. I told him that I was always busy. It was too fast and too strange. Besides, if he had not been married, he would have asked me out in South Benton.

Leslie was disgusted with me. She said I really blew it. I should have given him my phone number. That might have been my one and only chance to meet someone. Tomorrow I will put a sign out in front of mother's house that says: "If you are Hungarian and work at Sears and have a son who will enter Mason State, please call American English teacher who is divorced with two children at Mason State. The number is Middletown 1-317-0000000." I wish I were crazy enough to put the sign out. Maybe, just maybe, he was divorced or widowed and couldn't admit it. There will always be another yard sale. Maybe the mysterious foreigner will walk into my life and take me away to some romantic world. He walked in but I shut the door. You are a tough act to follow, Andrew, because I have this impossible hangup of only remembering the good things about our marriage. Will I ever be able to properly hate you? I hope so. I hope it will be soon.

Love,
Adrianne

June 22, 1974

Dear Andrew,

I am faced with a growing problem. Remember those little scrawny sticks we stuck in the ground all around the yard hoping someday they would grow into a pretty hedge? They grew and they grew and they grew. They grew past the stage of being a pretty hedge and into the stage of being a long, tall jungle. I tried ignoring them but they have gotten beyond the place where they can be ignored. Those tiny sticks have grown up to be nine feet tall with a definite weight problem. The stems, stalks, or trunks are thicker than my thumb, and I happen to have a very hefty thumb.

The electric hedge trimmers won't dent the jungle. It means buying some of those special cutters and actually cutting the hedge down to a normal size by cutting each stem. Three sides of the yard are covered by this forest of hedge and forsythia bushes. I guess it will be my summer project. When the children were small I would have given anything for a thick hedge so that we would have had some privacy. Now it is simply a nuisance. If I ever get it hacked down to a workable height, I will be able to keep it trimmed with the electric trimmers.

It used to be fun for us to work in the yard as a family. Now it is a nightmare to keep up with the grass, weeds, and the monster hedge. I would hire someone to do it but no one does yard work for less than a fortune an hour. It's the little things around here that you used to do that I miss the most. Things fall off, and I don't know how to put them back on. I have this horrible feeling that I am trapped in a house that will crumble around me before I ever get it paid off. If I could do it over, I would never read Shakespeare's plays. I would have enrolled in shop and mechanic classes. If possible, instead of college, I would have spent time as a plumber's assistant and an electrician's helper. Book learning is fine but a sonnet doesn't make the home repairs. Why are women so helpless when it comes to home repairs? Even the yard work fights me. I suppose I could call you and see if you would be interested in some starts from the hedge. I guess it would be a friendly thing to do but I doubt if wife number two would approve. I miss your muscles around the house in many ways.

Love,
Adrianne

Dear Andrew,

People joke about obscene phone calls. I don't ever remember a truly obscene phone call while we were married. We used to have students once in a while call to mess around, but there was never anything really filthy. Tonight it was a different story. I picked up the phone and there was this weird voice saying what I have never heard said before. I was shocked but not enough to hang up. I kept listening.

The voice was too mature for a student but it was not a voice that I recognized. I started breathing heavily into the phone. I thought it might encourage him to continue talking. It did. Then I decided to brazen it out so I said: "Stop talking about it and get over here on the double." This must have taken him by surprise because the next thing I knew, he shouted: "What are you, some kind of a pervert?" Then he hung up before I could answer him.

It makes me feel a little insecure to realize that I can't even cope with an obscene phone call in the proper manner. Maybe he will call back and I can hang up. I didn't think he would be rude since I was trying to be friendly. Maybe that is my problem. I must be too friendly to the wrong people. I should have learned that from having been married to you. I always tried to be friendly and pleasant to you and all that got me was a broken heart and a divorce. Will this madness ever end? How much more will I endure before I find some relief from the loneliness and the insecurity that the divorce has left me with? I desperately miss the security of my marriage.

P.S.   Was that you who called?

Love
Adrianne

Dear Andrew,

Having looked in the mirror, I decided that I look like the blob that ate Cincinnati. I can't even believe that I have gained so much weight. Nothing fits and I don't even care. Given the choice of eating everything in sight or trying to diet so I can get back into my school clothes, I vote for food. I am doing nothing but feeding my frustrations.

This is the most I have ever weighed in my life. If I continue at this rate, I will weigh as much as my mother. I did quite well after the divorce. I lost enough weight so that I looked like a human being. Then, instead of being lonely and not eating, I started being lonely and eating everything in sight. I have got to do something before school starts or I will be the only teacher who rolls to class. I don't have a single school outfit that I can get into without splitting a seam. I guess I'll have to buy some larger sizes. Right now the only fun I have is eating out, eating in, or eating all the time. I went the route of being thin and attractive, and no one could have cared less. At least this way I do enjoy the food that I eat. Fat is beautiful! Flaunt your flab! Pig people unite! Who knows, maybe I can pose for a new series of fat nudes. Rita in the Raw seemed to be successful. Then there is always a summer job with the circus. If I can't do anything else right, at least I can successfully gain weight. Which reminds me, I think I'll have a piece of cake. Maybe I'll have the whole cake!

Heavily,
Adrianne
Love,

July 12, 1972

Dear Andrew,

I wish I were dead. The depression is back.

Love,
Adrianne

July 13, 1974

Dear Andrew,
    I am in a black funk mood. I still wish that I were dead.
Love,
Adrianne

P.S.   This summer mother says she will pay for the gun if I will stop moping around and use it.

July 15, 1974

Dear Andrew,
    Leslie is nineteen. I married you when I was nineteen. Now I am sure that I wish I were dead.
Desperately,
Adrianne

July 16, 1974

Dear Andrew,
    If I can't be dead, I wish I were able to smile and mean it. This is worse than the summer after the divorce. I feel so lost.
Love,
Adrianne

July 25, 1974

Dear Andrew,
    My mood is very low. Mother sensed it and has been spending her vacation with Leslie and me. So far it has been a disaster. Usually we can entertain each other by going to auctions but this time things have been impossible For the first time all summer, there have been very few auctions advertised. We went to one, and they didn't have any antiques or any collector's items or even anything of interest. Then we drove to Hagerstown the following day

and got there early. We found the place where the auction was supposed to be, but there were no signs of auction activity. Other people were arriving and waiting but still there was no sign of any auction.

Since we had plenty of time before the auction was to start, Mother and I decided to walk around the town a little. We found an antique shop and went in. While we were looking around we discovered that the auction had been cancelled. As a matter of fact, the woman at the shop had bought most of the items that were to have been auctioned. It was a most unusual situation. This doesn't happen very often. I suppose we will never hear all the details as to why the auction did not take place. So this auction turned out to be a waste of time.

Our favorite auctioneer, Clinton, had one scheduled for today in Raymont, Indiana. There wasn't a great deal advertised but half an auction is better than none when you are hooked on auctions. Leslie had plans with Mark, so Mother and I had decided to drive over early. At least going to an auction gave us something to do. This summer is very difficult for me. I think it is the worst I have experienced since the divorce. I should be getting better but instead, I am more and more depressed. I try not to show it but there is a growing sense of terror inside me. I want to find an end to everything. Running away or suicide look very attractive. I keep fighting the feeling but sometimes I am obsessed with the desire to give up. I suppose I should go back to the doctor but since he has problems of his own, it doesn't seem to help much. When I see him with the same zombie look deep within his eyes, it is hard to believe the words that he hands out. His quick marriage may have been a little too quick. Seeing a doctor is not the answer. I do know there has to be a break in my mood before long.

There were two auctions advertised on this day. We drove by the first one on the way to Raymont. It was the most nothing that I had ever seen. We still had plenty of time but we went on to the auction in Raymont. As usual

I looked charming in my favorite old blouse and shorts. I have gained so much weight that I fill every seam to perfection. With Mother at two hundred and fifty and me getting close, we must look like Tweedle Dee and Tweedle Dum from *Alice in Wonderland.*

By the time we got to the house where the auction was to be held, everything was set up. Clinton is our favorite auctioneer. He auctions fast and he is fun. Also, he is the right size. Bill Clinton must weigh three-fifty or four hundred pounds. We have been attending his auctions for over a year and mother and I both enjoy him. He is corny but it is a nice kind of corny. Mother and I also manage to get some good buys, so that keeps us returning. One reason his auctions run so smoothly is because he has a good setup crew. He has a crazy, hot-tempered Italian who gets everything setup. Nick is quite a character. I like to watch him. He knows what he is doing, and he doesn't take any nonsense off anyone. He probably belongs to the Mafia. I notice that when he speaks, the people around him listen.

We have been to so many auctions for Clinton that his workers all recognize Mother and me. Actually, I should say they know Mother. She is the one who does most of the buying. I go along to keep from cracking up. Today everything was pretty well setup. Nick was sitting down when we walked up. Mother started talking to him. Nick said there wasn't too much in the way of antiques. A child's doll bed, a roseback chair, and a few pieces of china. Mother collects cups and saucers, so she went over to check the china. Since it was so hot, Nick asked me to go get him a beer. I thought he was kidding so I didn't pay much attention.

Mother decided to stay because they had one good cup and saucer that she wanted to bid on. They also had some kitchen appliances that we might be able to pick up for Leslie. (We will soon have Leslie's kitchen all equipped if we keep going to enough auctions.) There was still a good hour before the auction, so Mother and I decided to go get a Coke before it started. I told her when we got to the car that Nick had asked for a beer and that I had half a notion to get him one. Nick has always been nice about helping us load stuff in the car. Besides, if someone asks me to do something within reason, I usually do it.

Mother and I had a Coke. Then I pulled into a Pizza Queen and went in for some cold beer. I am so dumb about alcohol I didn't even know what kind to ask for. The girl thought I was a real dud when I asked her what kind of beer was best. She rattled off about six or eight different kinds. I told her to give me one that I had heard advertised on television. I get embarrassed asking to buy beer. I think that everyone in the place thinks I am an alcoholic.

We drove back to the auction and I put two of the beers in a sack and took them up to Nick. I felt like super fool. He had been teasing. He doesn't even drink beer. Mother, being her usual tactful self, told him that since her daughter had lowered herself to go in and buy them, that he had better drink them. It was an awkward situation but he seemed genuinely touched that I had taken the trouble to do him a favor. Maybe people don't always return his favors either.

It seems as if the world is divided into people who give and people who take. I classify myself as a giver. As I remember our marriage, you were a taker. That was one of the problems. I know I always gave, and you always took. You were the only person that I ever knew who could drive into a filling station with the children and me and while you waited for gas you would buy one Coke for yourself. I always thought this was a little strange. I wonder if there will ever be a time in my life when someone gives to me? Only time will tell.

I guess I should be thankful that you gave me my freedom but that wasn't exactly a precious gift. At least I have not yet learned to appreciate it as much.

Love,
Adrianne

Dear Andrew,

Veterinarian bills should have been covered as part of the divorce agreement. If I got custody of the dogs, you should have been responsible for their medical bills. They are younger members of the family and deserve equal treatment. Snoopy has been acting strangely for quite a while. Today the vet told Leslie and me that Snoopy has what they call the dachshund syndrome, which is a characteristic weakness in the dog's back that can get so bad the dog would have to be put to sleep. Here I am with the divorce syndrome and no one offers to put me to sleep.

Leslie was not ready to face anything like that. The tears welled up in her eyes. I thought she was going to break down right there. Then the vet told her that we might have caught Snoopy in time to put him on a corrective program of medication, special diet, and limited activity. I can't believe that this is happening. Now I am paying a vet bill of fifteen dollars a month for vitamins, shots, and so forth.

That is only the beginning. The vet informed us that dog food was the worst thing we could feed Snoopy. He needed vegetables, eggs, cottage cheese, meat, and cereal. The dog now has a higher standard of nutrition than I do. But wait, it gets better. We had to buy a used playpen to keep Snoopy in for at least six weeks. He must not jump up and down on the furniture. When he goes outside, someone has to carry him up and down the steps. If we watch Snoopy's diet, give him his medicine, and keep him from being too active, we may be able to keep him alive. Of course, this will cost at least ten dollars a month for medicine the rest of his life.

My first impulse was to drop Snoopy in a plastic bag and seal it shut. It would be a lot cheaper, but I can't do it. That dog means too much to Leslie. I never will forget the afternoon you were watching a basketball game on television. Leslie showed you the advertisement in the paper for a male dachshund that was six weeks old. You turned off the television set and took her out and bought the puppy. Those are the times that she remembers about her father. Her puppy is a part of those times. That dog is very special because he was your present to her. I suppose if it cost fifty dollars a month I would pay it to keep her dreams of her father alive.

So we got Snoopy started on the medicine. We stopped and bought him his own carton of cottage cheese. Now we are trying to find a used playpen. Mark is going to build a ramp by the steps so Snoopy will be able to get up and down more easily. I hope all these preparations and precautions work. I know that Leslie would be crushed if anything happened to that dog.

I must, however, remember that during my next divorce that I make sure there is a clause that covers medical expenses for pets. That should be a major item. Send donations! I am not too proud to accept them. Maybe you would like to come over and visit Snoopy. We are going to setup visiting hours for friends and former husbands.

Love,
Adrianne

P.S.   If you think divorce has caused me to go to the dogs, you are right.

August 9, 1974

Dear Andrew,
This summer is one bad auction after another. Mother and I are both disappointed. We don't mind not being able to buy, but we do like to watch and listen. Lately there have been very few auctions and none with any good antiques. This afternoon there was another Clinton auction advertised in Raymont. So once again we decided to drive over.

It was quiet on the way. Mother and I have been together so much lately that we have run out of things to say to each other. I found myself driving and praying for something to happen that would snap me out of this horrible depression that I felt myself slipping into. I couldn't bear the thought of school starting at the end of the month. There was no way that I was ready to go back into the classroom. Part of teaching is offering hope and help to students. If there was no hope for my future, how could I help students? I find myself praying more than I used to, particularly when I drive. I was trying to explain to God that I had gone as far as I could alone, and that I was going to have to have help or I wouldn't be able to make it. I had made an appointment with the doctor for next week but I didn't think there would be any magic answer there.

The auction was nearly set up. Nick was inside when we got there. Mother and I looked around at the furniture. There were several beautiful pieces but I felt sure that they would bring a pretty high price. The one lady's chair was fantastic. I really enjoy looking at lovely furniture. Scott and I are both fascinated by chairs. Chairs don't sell well in the shop but we keep buying them. We were the only people outside at this auction. It is ridiculous to get there so early, but you never know what you may find. If it is a large auction you need time to look at all the items. You need time to check the condition of the item before you bid on it. You never want to bid unless you know what kind of shape the item is in. If you get the bid and buy it, it is too late to turn it back in. I have made enough mistakes that I write from experience.

Once again I was wearing my auction blouse and my favorite shorts. My hair was a mess and, in all, I must have resembled hog salad. When Nick came out of the house, he had an armload of books. He said hello to Mother and called me over to look at the books. Since I was a school-teacher, he knew that I often bid on books. There were a couple that were interesting but nothing spectacular. Since Mother, Nick, an old man, and myself were the only ones in the yard, we were all talking to make idle conversation. Mother was toward the back of the yard looking at some boxes of junk. That's what she likes best.

The old man asked Nick if I was his wife. I was surprised when Nick said yes. I must have registered my surprise because he looked at me and said: "What's the matter, wouldn't you want to be my wife?" I kind of shrugged and said, "Why not?" Before I realized what was happening, he had put his arms around me and kissed me. I couldn't believe that he had kissed me right there in a public place. I must have looked stunned because he simply pulled me back into his arms and kissed me again. I was embarrassed. I didn't know if Mother had seen what had happened or not. I guess I wished the ground would open up and swallow me. I knew my face must have been flaming red.

Nick laughed and said: "What's the matter? Don't you like to be kissed?" I blurted out: "Of course I do!" Then I really was embarrassed. Nick just went on with his work. The old man was sitting there chortling. I pulled myself together and walked down where Mother was standing. I prayed she had not seen what had happened. There was no way I could explain what had happened or why it had happened. I was completely flabbergasted by the whole experience. I had resolved myself into believing that I would never be kissed again as long as I lived. Then out of nowhere a madman grabs me and kisses me. I needed time to get my thoughts together.

I told Mother I had seen enough of the auction. We were close to the downtown area and had over an hour before the auction started. There was no way that I was going to stay in that yard. Nick had gone inside and I was glad. I had no idea of what he might do next. I didn't want to wait to find out. Mother and I walked uptown and looked in some of the stores. If she had seen what happened she didn't make any comment. This made me think she had not seen what happened because she usually doesn't refrain from some timely word of advice.

A million thoughts went through my mind. Why did Nick kiss me? I kept asking the question over and over but it didn't find an answer. About five minutes before the auction was to start we walked back. As soon as we got there, Nick yelled: "Where did you and your Mother disappear? I was going to buy you both an ice cream cone!" I told him we had gone to do some shopping. He smiled and said: "I'll buy you one next time." I smiled back. It felt good to smile at someone.

The prices went pretty high at the auction, and it seemed that Nick kept smiling at me. This was ridiculous because he always smiles at everyone. Mother and I bought two small tables and left before the auction was over. After I loaded the stuff into the station wagon, I looked back at the auction and to my surprise, Nick waved. I waved back and got into the car to drive home.

I wonder, Andrew, if you would be jealous to know someone else had kissed me. It was a very nice kiss. I wonder what it meant. Why do I think everything has meaning? Nick is such an unpredictable person he probably doesn't even remember kissing me. Still, it was nice to be kissed again. I always liked to be kissed, and I guess I have missed it. Tonight I think I'll dream of Nick instead of you.

Love,
Adrianne

August 12, 1974

Dear Andrew,

Mother has gone back to South Benton. I miss her in some ways but in others it is nice to not have to worry about entertaining her. I am afraid her vacation wasn't much fun. She should have taken it this week because now the good auctions have started again. It seems like we never

184

plan our vacation time correctly. This week there is an auction listed for almost every evening. Some of the ones listed sound like interesting ones.

Clinton had one at Connersville tonight, and I didn't know whether to attend or not. I have gone to auctions alone, but somehow, since Nick kissed me, it seems a little different. I am being silly—I can't stop thinking about that kiss. I tried to get in touch with Scott to see if he would go with me. I was a little pleased that he had made other plans. Since it was an evening auction, I decided to wear a pants suit and look halfway human. I don't ever remember dressing up to go to an evening auction. It has been a long time since I have wanted to dress up. Now I am sorry that I have added all this weight. I need to take some of it off before school starts, or I won't be able to wear my clothes. Today I start dieting.

I wondered if Nick would notice that I looked fairly decent. I did't want to be obvious so I decided to get there a little late. I wasn't quite prepared to see him alone. There I was making something out of nothing. That guy is so crazy he probably spends his life kissing girls. Nick probably likes to see the startled look on their faces. Maybe that was his way of paying for the beer. How am I supposed to understand Italians? He is the first one I have ever met. The way he kisses, I hope he isn't the last one that I meet. Maybe I should save my money and fly to Italy. If one crazy Italian kissing me for no reason at all can make me feel this good, imagine being turned loose in a whole country full of them. Wow! What a lovely way to go! It would sure beat hell out of the last couple of years of nothing.

My timing is terrible. I got to the city of Connersville too early. I drove downtown and got a cup of coffee. There was no way that I was going to be the first person at the auction. When I got there I was not alone; there was an enormous crowd. I saw the other auctioneer, and so I stopped to talk to him. I asked him if there were any good cups and saucers. I always watch for them, since Mother collects them. About that time someone put his arm around me. I must have really jumped. I looked around and there was Nick laughing his fool head off. We talked a few minutes about the antiques and then he had to get back to work. Nick seemed pleased to see me, but then he is pleased to see everyone.

I like to watch Nick because he finds such pleasure in life. That's the part of the divorce that I have been unable to understand. I always had a bubble of life inside me that made each day seem exciting no matter what happened. That's the part of me that I lost, and I can't seem to get it back. Maybe that is what attracts me to the Clinton auctions. I like to watch Nick because he is so very much alive. He seems to glow with vitality. His zest for living is beautiful. I hadn't realized how much time I spent watching him. I must be trying to see what makes him so full of life. I may be hoping that some of it will rub off. I know that I envy him, and I miss the way I used to be. So many maybes!

I don't know what I expected but I was a little let down when nothing at all happened. I stayed to the end of the auction and checked out. I hadn't bought much but I had enjoyed myself. Nick smiled at me several times but that was all. So much for romantic dreams! He didn't carry me off at the end of the auction. I was only another member of the crowd. Still the memory of the kiss was nice. No one can take that away. Oh, Andrew, I still miss you but at least someone noticed I was a woman.

Love,
Adrianne

Dear Andrew,

Imagine my surprise when I answered the phone today and heard a man's voice. Men don't call me, so I was astonished to find out it was Nick. He wanted to know if I planned to be at the auction in Raymont tomorrow night. I said that I had planned on it. He wanted to know if I was going to bring my son or my mother. I told him I did not know for sure about my son. I knew Mother wouldn't be there because she was back in South Benton.

Then he said that if I didn't bring my son, maybe we could get a bite to eat after the auction. I said that would be fine. Then he said good-bye, and I was more confused than ever. I can't believe that anyone would want to go out with me—I have gained too much weight, and I look terrible. Now I would have to worry about what to wear. I had another problem: I had already asked Scott to go with me. Now how do I tell my son I don't want him along because he might cramp my style?

The best way to tell Scott is straight out. So I drove up and took him out for supper. He didn't seem surprised to hear that Nick had called me. I guess one time when Scott was helping Nick setup some stuff at an auction, Nick had asked about his father. Scott had told him that we were divorced. Scott decided that he had other more important things to do than go to the auction at Raymont; one nice thing about an older son is the fact that he takes a hint without any trouble. I am not sure I appreciated his helpful hint about checking with Planned Parenthood to be sure I wouldn't get pregnant. A woman my age does not need a lecture from her son on birth control. About now I sometimes think my mistake was in not using birth control before he was born. Oh well, he meant well and I imagine it is funny to watch your mother be in a twitter over a date. After my experience with Scott, I didn't know if I would be able to say anything to Leslie about a date. I wasn't sure what she might say.

Then I figured, what the heck! I have always told the kids the truth and this was not the time to stop. I told her I might be late getting back from the auction because Nick had called me and asked me to get a sandwich after the auction. Leslie was excited for me. Leslie thought it was

187

great. She calls him Big Nick from the Mafia. She remembers him from some of the auctions that she had been to with me. I didn't realize how much the children wanted me to find a companion. I am glad they aren't upset. I didn't know what to expect in the way of a reaction—they are so anti-Peg that I didn't know what they would think if I decided to date someone. I suppose this is a little different. My home is already broken up. Peg successfully took care of that, right? Enough of you and Peg—my own life has taken a turn for the better. Maybe not for the better, but at least something different is happening. I can't imagine what Nick and I will talk about. I will be in agony until the auction is over.

Love,
Adrianne

August 14, 1974

Dear Andrew,

This has to be worse than a first date. I spent the morning wishing that I had told Nick I would not be at the auction in Raymont. I spent the afternoon trying to decide what to wear and wondering if I should have taken Scott along. I was too fat for my dresses and a dress would have looked strange. I had never worn a dress to an auction before. The auction didn't start until five-thirty. I prayed that it would be a short one. It was probably the most exciting auction of the summer and all of a sudden I couldn't care less about antiques.

Some older woman had put her Victorian antiques in storage some thirty years ago and tonight they were taking everything out and auctioning the things off. They didn't know exactly what they might find until they got started. I had wanted to be there early but then I couldn't take the thought of talking to Nick before it started. I got there and instead of going to the auction I walked uptown and looked around. I got back to the auction about half an hour before it started.

There was enough stuff there for three auctions. The crowd was enormous. I knew this was the wrong time to go out for supper. Nick saw me and came over to talk to me. He said there was a great deal more stuff to be auctioned off than what had been anticipated, and that he hoped I didn't mind eating late. I said it would be fine. At least he didn't want to break the date! now all I had to worry about was getting through the auction and being able to think of something to talk about.

They had the crowd move outside the warehouse for the auction. They held the articles for sale up in the air and took the bids. I know they were selling fabulous antiques but I couldn't keep my mind on the bidding for very long at a time. I did get a rose-back rocker out of tiger maple. Then I had to take it back to the car. There must have been over thirty signed cut-glass bowls, cut-glass vases, cut-glass lamp shades and lamps, and cut-glass assorted dishes. Before they were finished I was sick of the word cut-glass. Ten o'clock came. Eleven o'clock came. Twelve o'clock came, and they still auctioned. It was the latest evening auction I had ever been to. By the time it ended at twelve thirty I must have looked terrible. I knew my makeup was off. I was hot and sticky, and there was a strong chance that my deodorant had failed.

Nick asked me where I was parked and said he would meet me over there. That gave me a chance to freshen my makeup and comb my hair. Then I noticed that when I had moved the rocker so that it wouldn't poke me in the back of the head I had gotten a streak of dirt across my hand. I nearly panicked. It wouldn't wipe off. So there I was, as dry as a cottonmouth, trying to find enough spit to give my hand a spit bath. Not sanitary but effective!

About the time I was ready to drive off and forget the whole thing, Nick pulled up in his orange truck. I got out and locked the door of my car. I figured we would go off in his truck and pick my car up later. I figured wrong. His front seat was full of stuff so he said that we would eat at the Country Kitchen which was on my way home. I could drive over and then we wouldn't be coming back and forth the rest of the night. I turned to get back in the car, and I died. My car keys were locked inside. Nick started off slowly, and I started frantically waving him back. I hoped he would back over me with the truck so I didn't have to tell him that my keys were locked in the car.

He laughed and said he could take care of it. It took him only a few minutes to park his truck and come over to my car. I don't know what he did to my vent window but he got it open and then opened the door. It didn't bother him a bit but I felt like I was about ten years old and mentally incompetent.

Somehow I managed to get to the restaurant. I thought that the worst had to be over. I parked and got out as he was coming over my car. He was smiling and laughing at me. Now I had left my lights on. Nick teased me and said I was acting like one of my students instead of the teacher. He was right. I felt like I was sixteen and on my first date. One thing about Nick, he made me relax and smile. That was good because I needed to smile.

We went into the restaurant and ordered. By that time Nick was starved and ready for a steak. I told him I was going to settle for a salad. He thought it was a good idea because he knew I was getting fat. Then he gave me a lecture on taking care of myself so I wouldn't get as heavy as my mother. It was nice to have someone seem to care about me. The time went very fast, and I didn't have to worry about the conversation. Nick talked to me, the waitress, and everyone around. He simply didn't know a stranger. I enjoyed it very much. The meal ended too quickly, and it was time to leave.

Nick walked me back to the car and opened the door for me. I assumed it would be good-bye and see you at another auction. It must have been close to two in the morning. Instead of sending me on my way, he slid in next to me. We talked briefly and the next thing I realized was that we were necking like a couple of teenagers. It was beautiful! I continued to feel like one of my students, and I loved it. There is absolutely nothing like necking passionately, after three years of abstaining, to make a woman feel like a woman again. I enjoyed it so much that I did not even get embarrassed until I was driving back to Middletown. Then I had a lot of emotions that I wasn't ready to handle. Nick and I finally stopped necking, and he said he would call me so that he could come to Middletown and take me out to dinner. Then we said goodnight and I started back to Middletown.

On the way back I knew I was blushing. I knew that I was embarrassed. I was concerned that Nick would think badly of me for behaving that way on the first date. Then I said to heck with the guilt and the embarrassment. I felt too good. All of a sudden I knew I was alive and I liked it. Even if he never called or came to Middletown, Nick made me realize that there was a lot of living to be done. At least I had been kissed again and liked it, and I couldn't help but think that Nick had thoroughly enjoyed himself, too.

Somehow the trip back to Middletown went rapidly. I might be forty, but as Mehitabel always said, "Toujours gai, toujours gai, Wot the hell, Wot the hell, There's a dance in the old dame yet!" Mehitabel was so right. Now all I had to do was to explain to my daughter why I was so late in getting in from a date. I hoped that she would understand that it was a very late auction. Tonight, Andrew, I hope you are a little bit jealous.

Toujours gai,
Adrianne

P.S. I can't believe his curly hair! I may learn to speak Italian—pizza, lasagna, spaghetti, antipasto—that's a romantic language I could eat up! I'm smiling and I love it!

August 15, 1974

Dear Andrew,

A hickie! I'm forty years old and last night I got my first hickie. When I looked in the mirror and saw my neck I almost died. I wasn't worried about explaining to my daughter why it was the wee hours of the morning when I came in from my first date with an impetuous Italian, but explaining a hickie is entirely another matter. When I think of the number of times I have yelled at her for having a hickie. There is no way that I can explain this.

I decided that I wouldn't even try. Thank goodness for makeup. I will put on some makeup and wear a collar today. Would you believe I am still feeling and acting like a high-school student? What a lovely way to feel! Somehow I'm glad there is a hickie this morning. Now I am sure last night was real. Maybe I needed something so that I wouldn't think last night was some fantasy that I had made up to console myself.

A hickie! You have to admit it is a little funny. At least it is going to be a different relationship with Nick. In all the years I knew you, I never had a hickie. I guess it is an experience every woman should have. Thank goodness school isn't in session. Imagine trying to teach in a high school with a hickie on my neck. It would totally freak out every student I had. As it is, I think I have had my mind blown for the first time.

Love,
Adrianne

August 24, 1974

Dear Andrew,

School started for the teachers today, and I was ready. Seeing Nick has done me a lot of good. Some of his joy of living has rubbed off, and I feel more like myself than I have for several years. It's great to notice the good things around me. All of a sudden, I am eager to get back into the class-

192

room. There are many things that I have to teach, and this year I won't settle for less than doing my best.

The teachers were all glad to see me, and I could tell they were glad to see me smiling. It was a long time without a real smile and I am glad it is back. I want to run and and jump and roll down hillsides like a little kid. It's like getting over measles or mumps or some long illness. You feel like you have missed so much that you can hardly wait to try everything.

I hope this mood lasts because it means so much to me. I can even say that I hope things are going well for you. There is a possibility that losing you might not be the end of the world. In a strange, crazy way, it might be the beginning.

Tenderly,
Adrianne

P.S. I didn't have to worry—the hickie was gone, but not the memory.

August 31, 1974

Dear Andrew,

The summer has been moving at a rapid pace. All of a sudden I had to get ready for school and for life at the same time. It was an exhilarating feeling. Let's be honest, hearing from Nick and seeing him has been a real ego trip. He has a beautiful way of making me feel special. I have never known anyone who worried about my wishes. Nick is honestly concerned with what makes me happy. This is a new experience for me. I feel pampered, petted and appreciated. I adore it.

Leslie was there waiting for her date when Nick came for me. He made a great impression. They hit it off immediately. He thought she was sweet, pretty, not too fat, and probably abused by her mother. Leslie thought that he was exactly right. It wasn't any time at all until they were ganging up on me. Leslie had the most beautiful smile.

She needs to have someone to say nice things to her as much as I do. Nick has a magic smile that makes everyone feel better.

This evening Nick was wearing a good-looking sport coat. I liked it. He wanted to eat somewhere special so we went to Feeny's. I had checked with Scott, and Scott said they had antiques for decorations and the food was excellent. He was right. Nick liked it and I was pleased that he did.

The food was good and the conversation was even better. Nick liked the antiques that were used in the decorations. Nick's a very interesting person. All the time that I was married I don't remember when you and I ever really talked. Oh, we talked about the children, decisions, finances, and so forth, but we never talked about ideas. It seemed like I was always making the conversation and you had very little to say. I used to think it was boring but I never said anything. I thought that was the way a marriage was supposed to be.

With Nick it's completely different. Sometimes I say very little. It's nice to have someone talk to me about interesting things. He is serious and funny and very intelligent. The more I am with him, the more I respect him as a truly beautiful human being. I like his mad and unpredictable manner. I never know what he will say or do. It's great.

Even if my relationship with Nick turns out to be a few meetings filled with pretty words, it will have been the best experience that I have had in a long time. Somehow this wild Italian has put the magic back in my life. I will never be able to thank him enough. It is so good to want to be alive because living is a beautiful experience. I think I am going to make it. I hope so.

Love,
Adrianne

P.S. Yes, there is a second hickie but I won't say where!

Dear Andrew,

I feel fantastic. Things are going so well at school and with the children that I can't believe it. I want to smile and smile and smile. I want to laugh and laugh and laugh. I am even losing weight. I have shed fifteen pounds. I may become a beautiful butterfly who will live always in the sunshine.

No, Andrew, I am not drunk! I am glad to be alive.

Happily,
Adrianne

September 6, 1974

Dear Andrew,

This turned out to be a lovely evening. Nick had called me earlier in the week and said that he would like to come back to Middletown and to take me out for dinner. I was delighted. He said that I should select a place that would be interesting. In the last few years I have been to a hamburger stand, a taco place, and a family steak house. None of these were exactly what I thought he might have in mind. Feeny's had been a good choice the first time he came up. What could I plan this time?

I had a quick consultation with Scott, and he came up with several suggestions. I guess I am getting older when I have a son who comes on as the man about town. He went through a list of restaurants that I didn't even know existed. Scott finally settled on the Downtowner because it was new and still had excellent food.

When Nick came up I was ready for the evening. He looked nice but I had to laugh because he had driven his orange pick-up truck. I thought it was great. Maybe I should have suggested we go in my car but I liked the idea of going in the pick-up truck to eat at Middletown's newest and fanciest restaurant.

Scott's suggestion was excellent because Nick enjoyed the food and the ultrashort skirts of the waitresses. He

195

enjoyed gazing at the tops of their thighs, and I enjoyed gazing at him. We both enjoyed the food even though I stayed with a chef's salad. One thing about Nick is that he is honest and outspoken. He did not like the dress I was wearing and told me so. I didn't tell him that even though I had lost weight the number of dresses I could get back into was limited. I simply smiled and said that he would have to get used to the idea that I wear bright clothes. I do. He probably said it so I would order a salad. It was probably psychology on his part. It worked because a salad was what I ordered.

We had an interesting evening. I told Nick that my biggest problem was finding something to do that I liked. I'm not a sewer, nor a knitter, nor an artsy-craftsy person. He surprised me by saying: "You're an English teacher. Why don't you write a book?" For him it seemed a logical pattern of action. I've always thought about it. I guess instead of thinking about it, I should do it. Who knows? I might.

Nick has so many worthwhile things to say. He has traveled a lot and I like to listen to him. He made an interesting point. He said that women should only believe half of what a man promises her and then she would always be on the safe side. He is right. Nick is very perceptive for a high-school dropout. It bothers him that he doesn't have a high-school diploma and that I have five years of college. It doesn't bother me one bit. He has more wisdom from living than a lot of people that I know have with college diplomas. Sometimes caring about people is more important than having read the right list of books. I have the college degree but I am not sure that I have any wisdom at all. Anyway I told him that I would only believe half of his promises. Actually since I am divorced, I don't ask for any promises, and if they are volunteered, I don't count on them being fulfilled. I am afraid that you destroyed my ability to trust anyone for very long. But it was a lovely evening, and I liked being flattered and caressed. It's a great ego trip as long as I remember that it's a summer romance and that's all.

Love,
Adrianne

September 17, 1974

Dear Andrew,

Driving down the highway towards South Benton, I went through a large puddle of water. I was overtrained about stopping and trying my brakes so I became obsessed with testing my brakes. I had to wait for two cars to pass me. Then I tried my brakes and they were fine. I kept driving and noticed a truckload of aluminum canoes on a truck that was coming toward me. As I watched, the load of canoes broke loose and at least three of them came sailing through the air into my lane of traffic. I braked hurriedly to keep from being hit by them. Thank goodness nothing was in back of me, or they would have made it to the front of my car the hard way.

I couldn't believe that such huge canoes could come flying clear across the road. If I had been there a little sooner, they would have been through my front window. Now I am glad that I took the time to let the two cars pass me so that I could try my brakes. Otherwise, I might have been in the path of the flying canoes. Can you imagine my poor mother trying to explain to people that her only daughter had been killed when she was hit by a flying aluminum canoe while driving down a state highway? It sounds funny but it was a little too close for comfort. I would hate to be at my funeral with everyone snickering because of the funny way I died. If I die, I plan on doing it in a serious manner so that you will grieve slightly.

Love,
Adrianne

Dear Andrew,

Guidance counselors and student advisors have a lot to learn, particularly about our daughter. She has been dreading the thought of taking the freshman English class at Mason State. I told her to try and test out of it. I figured it would cost her five dollars for the test. Since her language pattern is basically sound, I felt she had a good chance of passing the test. She had to get the forms from her college student advisor. In the process, he told her that she was wasting her time and her money because her SAT scores were so low she couldn't possibly pass the test given by the Mason State English Department.

I am glad that she did not let him fake her out. She went ahead with her plans and took the test. She passed the test and got her four hours of college credit. It is so great to see how pleased she gets when she accomplishes something like that. I believe in time she may convince herself that she is intelligent.

The advisor couldn't believe she had passed the test. He made her feel good by telling her what a great accomplishment that was. I'm pleased that she is doing well. She has a nice way of working with people. This will be very important when she becomes a teacher. Oh, Andrew, you are missing some wonderful moments. I know I miss you desperately but at least I have the children. I can't believe that you have anything of value.

Proudly,
Adrianne

October 17, 1974

Dear Andrew,

Compassion is a word you no longer have in your vocabulary when it comes to our children. It may have seemed ridiculous to you that Scott wanted to stay overnight in the hospital when they cut out his wisdom teeth.

To me, it seemed like a natural request. Scott was scared. He felt like he would get better and less painful results if he were in the hospital. Since you pay the bill, you have the right to say where it will be done. I only wish that you were able to show a fatherly concern instead of a dollar concern. We always tried to provide the best for the children when we were a family. It is difficult for them to understand that you no longer want the best for them.

I hope it will give you a lot of pleasure to know that your son will be frightened and in pain so that you may save a few dollars. With a little bit of luck, maybe your teeth will drop out two at a time and bite holes in your throat.

Cheerfully,
Adrianne

October 20, 1974

Dear Andrew,

School is exciting this year. I like what we are doing with the Phase Elective English Program. I feel that as an English department we have some excellent and innovative ideas. The head of my English department and I have been attending meetings at Indianapolis and Kokomo. Some of the meetings are very rewarding and some of them are not worth the drive.

We attended one at Kokomo this afternoon. It was concerned with teachers from all over the state sharing ideas about the programs at their individual schools. I thought what we were offering at Sushawnee High School held its own with any in the state. I am pleased to be a part of it.

I was flattered when Mrs. Endicott from the State Department of Public Instruction asked me two things. She wanted me to write an article for the English newsletter concerning the money-making ideas that I have used for supplementing our tight budget. She also wanted to visit some of my classes. I told her that I was agreeable to both.

She will call me for a definite date to visit. She said she would let me know when she would like the article for publication. It doesn't take too much to make me happy. A pat on the head now and then is fine. Two pats on the head in one afternoon is fantastic.

Famously,
Adrianne

P.S. Make that three pats—Nick called!

October 24, 1974

Dear Andrew,

My mother is filled with helpful words. She keeps telling me not to date Nick. She believes that I will be hurt again. She may be right but I can't stop living because I get hurt. Part of accepting life is accepting the fact that if you live it you take the pain with the pleasure.

At this point I am totally selfish. I have had enough pain to last a long time and now I am greedy for pleasure. Seeing Nick gives me pleasure so I am going to continue seeing him. The only way that I will get hurt is if I start to believe all the promises that Nick might make. I don't think there will be a problem because I don't expect promises, and he doesn't make them. Whenever I tell him good-bye, I always think to myself: "Good-bye, Nick! If I never see you again I will always thank you for what you have done for me. No matter what the future brings, I will smile for you." Maybe it is silly and maye it is romantic nonsense, but I always think it. In my heart I seem to know that Nick is in my life to make me smile. Then he will go on about his life.

The way it is, if Nick and I get to the same auction we share a cup of coffee or a sandwich. It is nice when we get together. At other times we do our own thing. I don't ask a lot of questions about his life and he doesn't ask a lot of questions about my life. It is a situation where two adults enjoy each other's company when it is convenient. I like it that way, and I think he does.

I would like for mother to realize that if I get hurt again it is because I am stupid. I was hurt by you so I don't think I will ever plan on being stupid again. I keep telling Nick that a divorced woman only goes with a man for one reason. The first time I said it, he got mad. Now he laughs with me. That is the way it should be. The days of love, dove, and moon, June, croon are long past. Any relationship that I ever have again will be logical, rational, and convenient. I really don't want to love again.

Thoughtfully,
Adrianne

November 2, 1974

Dear Andrew,

Talking to you on the phone was a strange experience. It has been well over a year since I have heard your voice. It's always a bit of a shock to realize that I am actually talking to you. You surprised me. That's the first conversation since your marriage that didn't wind up in a shouting, swearing match. I think you were on your good behavior because you knew you were lying through your teeth.

There is no way that I will believe you had not received the statement for Leslie's Mason State University fees. I had mailed the statement myself. The envelope had my return address. Leslie was dropped from all her classes. I hope you get the fees paid so that she will be able to pick them back up. There wasn't any excuse for your not having paid them on time. If you had not received the statement, you should have called to check on it. I will solve future problems. Next time I will send the statement by registered mail, and then I will know that you receive it on time.

I was a little surprised when you called me at school and wanted to drop the check off at the house. You surprised me by wanting to join me for a cup of coffee. There would have been a time when I would have given anything for such an opening. That time is over. Talking to you on the phone is difficult enough. I am glad that I told you to drop it in the mail slot. I got in touch with Leslie, and she picked up the check and went out to Mason State. She got back into her classes so it was no big deal. Don't let it happen again. You must be counting pennies or you would have paid the book money on time. Your checkbook must not balance or you would not have to send the book money next week.

I won't nag about it. I am simply glad that we could work it out in an adult manner. That's the way it should have been from the beginning but you were hyper over everything.

Love,
Adrianne

November 7, 1974

Dear Andrew,

Once again Scott has created a situation that leaves me with mixed emotions. Since he is back at Mason State, he has become more and more involved and interested in antiques. Mother and I have helped him to buy enough stock so that he has become a full partner in the shop. So now he has made a decision. He is going to drop out of Mason State at the end of the fall quarter. He realizes that his grades have dropped, and he really isn't interested in college. For the past year, he has tried to buy antiques, refinish antiques, sell antiques, do antique shows in other cities, and attend college classes. This was a bad situation because he was doing a bad job of both.

Scott thought I might be upset but I am not. He was working on an English license and there is no way that he would ever be happy in a high-school classroom. With his grades dropping so low, if he did finish and get a license there wouldn't be a school sytem that would hire him. Right now with the on-again, off-again recession, he might as well spend all his time on antiques. That has been his first love for a very long time. Maybe he can make a go of it if he really concentrates all his efforts in developing the business of antiques. If he finds out that he has made a mistake, he can go back and pick up his scholarship. Then I am sure that if he goes back to college he would think it was worthwhile and then he could buckle down and bring up his grade point.

I hope his decision will be right for him. I think that is important for him to be doing something he likes. Life is too short to spend working at something you hate. I know he has been fascinated with antiques since the seventh grade. I think he has made the right decision. I wish he might have talked to you but at this point you two are still strangers.

Love,
Adrianne

November 24, 1974

Dear Andrew,

Thanksgiving was a disaster. Mother decided to spend the whole mealtime taking potshots at the children. They have not done anything right for the last few months, and she decided to tell them about it with Mark sharing the Thanksgiving meal. It was a lovely meal complete with turkey, dressing, mashed potatoes, sweet potatoes, cranberry sauce, salad, green bean casserole, hot rolls, pumpkin and apple pie. About halfway through the meal, she noticed that none of us were able to eat. She didn't even realize that she had spoiled all of our appetites.

When I started to let the water out of the kitchen drain, it wouldn't go down. It had been sluggish for several days, I but kept telling myself that this couldn't be happening on Thanksgiving Day It was happening. The whole drain system was clogged up. It wasn't a new situation for this old house, but in the past you were always here to help deal with it. Instead, Mark put on a pair of Leslie's old jeans and helped me. It meant taking the pipes under the kitchen apart and running the hose in and flushing the drain with water. It's a dirty messy job but it was easier to do it than pay a plumber fifty dollars or more, since it was a holiday. Mark and I finally got the section that was stopped up. We got it cleared out. Then Mark put the pieces of pipe back together and tightened them up. Mark doesn't say much but he is a good worker. Scott and Leslie were both so mad from what had happened during the meal that they stayed upstairs and pouted. Mark and I decided that we were having more fun playing with the smelly drain than being upstairs. We also decided that next year we were going to MacDonalds for Thanksgiving dinner. We couldn't take counting our blessings today.

Love,
Adrianne

December 1, 1974

Dear Andrew,

Scott has been living in a pretty rough neighborhood for the last month. I accepted the fact that he and Jeff would close the antique shop and do only antique shows but I had cautioned them about the neighborhood into which they had moved. I knew they would have problems so I told them how to go about getting insurance.

In his usual charming manner, he ignored my advice. Last night they were ripped off. He called to tell me that many of their personal antiques had been taken. A number of things that belong to Mother and me were taken. After he told me what was missing, he paused. Then he told me that he had not followed through on taking out the insurance. What do I say in a situation like that? Somehow a dismal: "Oh, no, Scott!" was not at all tension relieving. I should have at least said, "F——!" It might have helped. I'm sure that it would have been a word he understood. But then I guess mothers do not say those words to their sons.

I hope his next show will turn out to be a good one

because at this point he is not going to become rich. As a matter of fact, I think he made a major step backward to the category of poor. The worst part is that he is taking Mother and me along with him. I wonder if all divorced mothers have difficulty getting their sons to listen to anything that is at all sensible. I say it but somehow when it leaves my lips and hits his brain cells it gets lost or translated incorrectly.

One day very soon I am going to stop talking to him like an adult and hit him with a baseball bat. I feel terrible because so many things were taken but maybe tomorrow will be brighter. At least I'm not afraid of tomorrow.

Love,
Adrianne

December 6, 1974

Dear Andrew,

Mrs. Endicott from the State Department of Public Instruction drove to our little country high school to visit my class. She was interested in observing the one called: Me, Myself, and I. I was so pleased that she could come and visit. I thought perhaps when I had talked to her in Kokomo that she was only making polite conversation.

She stayed for the whole hour and seemed to be impressed with what the students and I were trying to do as a group. I wasn't sure how things would go because two of my best discussion people were on a field trip. I couldn't have asked for a more workable situation. As a class we were evaluating the Identity Collages that they had made two weeks earlier. In this particular class we are exploring how the individual relates to various problem situations that are found in the world of today. The problem situations vary with the interests of the class. We get into some pretty controversial areas but the students seem to like it.

The students do a lot of reading, writing, and basic communicating. There is a lot of idea exchanging. Students are encouraged to react honestly. Once we break the ice things go quite well. Today I had pushed all the tables and chairs back and we were sitting on the floor. For some reason the discussions go better when we get away from the tables and the formal situation. It's a little unorthodox for a country school but it works. I don't worry too much about routine as long as I get active student involvement.

Mrs. Endicott and I talked after the class. She was interested in what I was doing. She wanted a copy of the course of study. I am in the process of rewriting it, so she asked me to send one when it was completed. Sometimes it makes a teacher feel good to know that someone is interested in what she is doing in her classroom. I know I liked the feeling that someone appreciated my teaching ability. I was proud of my class today and I was a little bit proud of myself.

Love,
Adrianne

December 16, 1974

Dear Andrew,

To think that I had thought you had forgotten our son's twenty-first birthday. You really are sentimental. The representative from the sheriff's office gave me the summons. I couldn't figure out what it meant. I thought you knew that I understood you were no longer financially responsible for Scott after he reached the age of twenty-one. That was why I had written earlier to have you send me the information about his Blue Cross-Blue Shield policy.

I called my lawyer and read her the message on the summons. She informed me that you had spent $175 to set up a court date to affirm what the original divorce decree had set up. Since I understand that financial aid stopped, there was no point in my appearing in court. She said she would inform your lawyer and take care of the situation. It is hard for me to believe that you are such a dumb ass.

Wouldn't it have been cheaper to call me and ask if I were going to put up any type of fight? Even paying ten cents to call from a pay phone would have been cheaper than the $175 legal process. Maybe you got that much pleasure out of knowing that a summons would cause us some concern. Being the practical soul that I am, I wish you had called me and checked on it. Then if you had an extra $175 you could have given it to the children or to the shrine of St. Jude. The Dominican Fathers in Chicago could have prayed for all of us. This way it doesn't do anyone any good. If you have that kind of money to throw around, you might pay your bills on time. People are beginning to talk.

I am still sentimental today. I think of twenty-one years ago when you first saw your son. You were so proud of him. We couldn't wait to get him home so that we would be able to hold him and love him as much as we wanted. Now he is too big to hold, and I am the only one he knows that loves him. Being twenty-one is special for a young man. I am sorry you couldn't send him a note or call him. I took him out for supper. I liked knowing that he has grown up. Scott still has a lot to learn but he will make it and that is what is important. We didn't do too badly with him. Scott has a lot of good qualities. I wish you were able to share them. I think I can honestly say that in many ways your son is more of a man than you are. Time does strange things. I hope you remember your son today, and I hope you realize how much you have given up.

Love,
Adrianne

December 20, 1974

Dear Andrew,

One of the nicest parts about Leslie being engaged to Mark is the fact that he shares his Grandmother Hamilton with her. This has been a rewarding relationship for Leslie. If

I am late she can always stop by and visit with Grandma Hamilton. They can spend hours together and enjoy talking. It's good for Leslie because Grandma Hamilton is sharing recipes and ideas with Leslie. In return Leslie takes her to the grocery and to the doctor or the shopping center. They look after each other.

Their latest project is for Grandma Hamilton to teach Leslie how to crochet. Grandma Hamilton can crochet anything and it is a great experience for Leslie to learn. I would have liked to be a mouse and watch them. Grandma Hamilton is right handed and Leslie is left handed so they had a few adjustments to work out. It didn't take long until Leslie got the hang of it and she is well on her way to crocheting her first afghan.

That's what I envy most about Leslie. She is always busy doing something. She either cooks, sews, or crochets or studies. She stays occupied. I still have trouble finding enough projects to hold my attention. I probably spend more time grading papers than I do anything else. I think of all the things I could do but none of them seem to be of any lasting interest. I seem to enjoy writing as much as anything. I am still looking for other areas of interest. I should give Grandma Hamilton a real challenge and have her teach me how to crochet. I suppose it would help pass the time away. I do notice that I have less and less free time.

Love,
Adrianne

January 1, 1975

Dear Andrew,

Slowly I am becoming aware of a complete change in myself. Yes, I am sometimes lonely. Yes, I still miss the love we once shared. Those are facts that exist but now they are in the proper perspective. I'm discovering my identity. I am a person in my own right.

I have been attending English conferences and workshops all over the state. People are interested in what I have to say. My first article will be published in a statewide English newsletter. English teachers from other cities are writing to ask about some of my ideas. This is exciting and rewarding because it is happening to me.

With the new phase system of classes in English, I am developing new classes and new ways of sneaking up on students to teach them the fundamentals of reading and writing. People from the State Department of Education are coming in to watch. Best of all, the classes are elective and the students are signing up to take them. In some classes the enrollment has jumped from ten students to thirty-five students. This pleases me. I must be doing something right.

There are still many times when I am alone, but the house is no longer empty. I am busy with new ideas and new materials to keep English moving in the twentieth century. Often the loneliness is broken by the phone ringing. I am building a circle of friends who call to say: "Let's get a taco!" or "Let's go shopping!" or "Want to judge a speech meet?" Leslie and Scott are more relaxed and open. They are glad to see me because I am not desperate to be with them. I no longer panic at the thought of being alone. I am able to relax and be company for myself.

In the process of being married to you, I became "Andrew's wife." I lost my identity. It has taken me almost three years to discover that I am an independent person. I have built a new world, and I like it. It isn't perfect and it isn't finished but it is mine. One day soon, I won't need to write you any more letters.

Love,
Adrianne

P.S. Nick sent me a card for no reason. That's so much nicer than receiving one for a holiday.

January 5, 1975

Dear Andrew,

By mistake I received a bill for $117.39 from Dr. Gusto for dental work regarding Scott. When I called the office to see why I had received the bill, I discovered that they had sent it to me by mistake. This was the major part of the bill for when Scott had his wisdom teeth cut out. It seems that at this point you have only paid $20.00. I don't understand how a man who is making over twice my salary can be such a deadbeat.

I tried to be as helpful and understanding as I could. I told the secretary in the dentist's office that you were making over twenty thousand a year and were under a legal obligation because of the terms of the divorce to pay the bill promptly. I also gave her the name of your lawyer who might prompt you to rapid payment. In case that didn't work or was ineffective, I mentioned that a polite phone call to the city superintendent of public instruction would guarantee results.

Andrew, you should know by now that it doesn't do you any good to embarrass me by not paying the bills. I will always be a little nastier than you. That is part of the rules of divorce. You hurt me, and I hurt you. Pain is the name of the game, and I am learning to give as good as I get.

It was amazing how fast you paid the pathologist's bill for Leslie after the third time I mailed you the statement. It must have been the note on the outside of the bill's envelope which read: "Dear Deadbeat, Please pay the bill for five dollars, or I will try to organize a collection from your teaching staff to pay it." It's not fair, and it's not nice but it gets results. I don't like unpaid bills when the children and I have to be involved. Have a lovely day!

Love,
Adrianne

Dear Andrew,

Leslie was thrilled this evening. Nick would spoil her rotten with half a chance. Mark's folks had gotten her a ten-gallon tank for tropical fish for Christmas, and she loved it. Tonight Nick brought her a twenty-gallon tank, and she is thrilled about getting it all set up. To be honest, I am not that crazy about fish tanks but I can put up with them.

The best part of the gift was not that it was a fish tank but that Nick cared enough to bring her a present for no other reason than that he liked her. He wanted her to smile when she got it. Nick has never had any children of his own so Leslie has become rather special for him. She is the good part of a life that he missed. They seem to fill a need for each other, and it makes a special relationship. She smiled so sweetly. I am sorry that you are missing her smile and her happiness. She is quite a special young lady.

What a lovely relationship exists with Nick. He drops in without calling. He calls to hear my voice. He sends a card for no reason. He buys me a record album because he wants me to listen to the lyrics. For some reason he makes me feel that he is enjoying himself when he makes me happy. Sometimes I don't hear from him for weeks! Then I look up, and he is outside my classroom door. He never asks where I've been or what I have been doing. Nick accepts me the way he finds me and always seems happy when he finds me. Right now it is exactly what I need. It's a warm, friendly relationship with no promises on either side. When we are together it is good, and when we are apart we do our own thing. Nick has helped me to develop a healthy perspective on what is important in living. I'm even working on my writing. It won't be the great American novel but it might sell. At least writing keeps me busy in the lonely hours when I'm at loose ends. I am glad that Nick is my friend. I needed one.

I'm not ready to be serious about anyone and neither is he. I still have a long way to go but I am getting there.

At least I am beginning to feel like I am a person with an identity of my own. I am sure that my identity will change many times but at least I am beginning to know that I am a person on my own. I am learning to live two ways, alone and with people. Both ways are good within their perspectives. I think less and less about being Andrew's former wife and more and more about being Adrianne. I know this is good.

Thoughtfully,
Adrianne

January 8, 1975

Dear Andrew,

Today I got the state publication for English teachers in the mail. I was very pleased because they had published my article about raising funds for Phase Elective English. There was a certain thrill in opening the publication and realizing that the author of the article was myself. It looked so impressive in print. I have always enjoyed writing but it had been a long time since I had had anything published.

I was even more surprised when I came home this evening and discovered that the local newspaper had a paragraph about my article having been published. I couldn't help but be excited to know that all over Indiana English teachers would have a chance to read my article. Not only that but people all over Middletown would say: "I remember her. I used to ride the bus with her when she was taking classes at Mason State. She lives in our neighborhood. That's my son's teacher!" People will think of me as a person and this is good.

Being honest, I hope you saw it, and I hope you were proud of me. That way you will understand that I am going to be all right.

Proudly,
Adrianne

P.S. Nick was proud of me. He has the most fantastic smile.

January 10, 1975

Dear Andrew,

This is the type of situation that sneaked up on me and I didn't know whether to laugh or cry. Today I attended an auction. Nick was there. We were laughing and talking when Jonesy came up. Jonesy is the only name I know him by. He is another auction buff that I have noticed. Jonesy seemed happy to see Nick. I was only halfway listening to their conversation because I was waiting for a special cup and saucer to come up for bid.

Then I heard Jonesy say to Nick: "The wife and I were glad that you and Mary could come over for supper last night. Seems like we always have a good time when the four of us get together. Guess we are lucky to have such good wives." I wanted the ground to open and swallow me. In one moment the world ended, and my life went on. Nick went on talking to Jonesy in his own unique manner, and I forgot to bid on the cup and saucer. In the centuries that followed I felt numb all over. I suppose I should have cried or run away or done something dramatic but I stood there forever and ever and ever.

Jonsey finally moved away and Nick very quietly said: "I think we need to talk." Somehow I had the feeling that everything had been said. One thing about a divorce, it does keep you calm in unique situations. Nick and I left the auction and drove to a coffee shop. We talked for a long time. What I liked best about Nick was his ability to talk and to listen when something important was happening. I guess the kindest way to phrase what happened was to say that I was Nick's good deed. He had noticed me for a long time when I attended auctions. He is a very intuitive man and he was concerned about me. He knew that I was letting myself go and that I seemed more and more depressed. I think he realized how fine the line had been drawn between life and death. So he decided to do something about it. He thought that if I believed that someone cared about me as a person I would snap out of the depression. So he took a calculated risk by deciding to be the person who cared about me. He believed that if I got back into the swing of living, he could gradually move out of my life and back to his wife. It was a wild, impossible story but typical of what this man would do to help even a total stranger.

I suppose that I should be angry or hurt but I don't think I am. It was a crazy thing to do but it worked and for this I have to be thankful. Nick's smile was magic and his tenderness was most healing at a critical period in my life. For a short time, Nick and I shared a very special relationship. I never thought about us in terms of marriage so that part doesn't hurt. It doesn't make any sense and I am scarcely willing to believe it but I think I loved him. He was a beautiful person and he gave me some moments to remember without regret or sorrow but with a smile. I didn't think about the fact that he might have had a wife. I hope that I have not hurt his marriage in any way. I hope that his wife will never hear about me even accidentally. It would take a special type of wife to understand that to Nick I was a lost child or an abandoned kitten. He helped me and he would go on to help the next person by doing what he believed would have to be done.

Nick and I have said good-bye. My Italian episode is over. It was not the ending I might have chosen but it is one which I will be able to live with. I'll never again drive to Raymont to meet him, and he will never again drive to Middletown to meet me. If we see each other at an auction we have agreed that it will only be to smile and perhaps to remember. His smile, his kiss, and his touch was very special. I shall miss him. Yet, I can't help but think he will always be a part of my life. He gave me back my zest for living, and now it is my turn to share it with others. Nick was a crazy answer to a desperate prayer but I have never doubted that God works in mysterious ways. At least I am not giving up. I am only curious about what will happen next.

Love,
Adrianne

P.S. Nick still has the most fantastic smile and when I remember him, I too shall smile.

January 12, 1975

Dear Andrew,

Forgive me for laughing but it is my turn. One of the teachers from your building called to find out how to get in touch with Scott concerning some antiques. Since she was on the phone she had to make a few female cat comments, and I must say I thoroughly enjoyed them. Justice works in funny ways. Jane had to bring up little bits of gossip. She finally got around to the subject of you and Peg.

Wow! You really have changed. It is difficult for me to imagine that you and Peg or that you and anyone engage in shouting matches when you get angry. I remember you as always being calm. I wonder what happened to you after the divorce? You certainly did a complete change of personalities.

The best part was when Jane told me that Peg was getting fat. That was the sweetest news I have had in a very long time. There is a certain delightful pleasure in imagining that my former husband is married to a fat shouting shrew. You may have paid a price higher than I can imagine. I can only say I hope you are miserable because I think you deserve it. Of course I am prejudiced but I am also amused. I only hope that Peg keeps gaining weight until you can't stand the sight of her. With an incentive like that I am bound to lose another five pounds. I want the world to know that as she looks worse not only will I feel better but I will look better. Look out smaller dress size, here I come!

Love,
Adrianne

Dear Andrew,

Living on a teacher's salary is a miserable way to live. There is never quite enough to take care of the necessities let alone any of the luxuries. I should have become a call girl or a waitress so that I would be able to live in the manner to which I would like to become accustomed. As it is, I sit around trying to come up with get-rich schemes. I have the ideas but I never know how to carry them through.

Today I thought about developing a Man of the Month Club. People could join it by paying a flat fee for a year. Once they paid the two hundred and forty dollar fee, they would receive a package in a plain brown wrapper. All they would have to do is open it, pour water over the dehydrated contents of the package, and there would be a full-size virile male who would be charming, delightful, and very, very obliging for twenty-four hours.

The receiver of the package would have twenty-four hours of pleasure and absolutely no danger of scandal, germs, or pregnancy because at the end of the time, the man would simply self-destruct. If the person would be a real swinging lady, she could receive a special weekly rate. The idea has endless potential. There is only one problem. I can't get the chemistry teacher to come up with the right formula for the dehydrated man. The best results to date turned out to be a box of brownies with nuts. It does seem that I come up with great ideas. Now why can't I find someone to put them into practice?

If I ever perfect this idea, I may even branch out into the Woman of the Month Club. Then I could send you a gift subscription and really upset you because you would rather be a member of the Man of the Month Club. A woman a month would be more than you could handle in any manner.

Sarcastically,
Adrianne

216

Dear Andrew,

Walking into the teacher's lounge this morning was not the most pleasant experience I have ever had. One of the teachers greeted me with the comment: "I saw Scott has made the newspaper." I didn't know that Scott had, so I made the simple-minded mistake of asking why he had made the newspaper. She explained that he had been to court on a charge of drunken driving. I hardly knew what to say. It was hard to believe I had not been told anything about it by Scott. Surely he knew I would hear about it from someone.

It is difficult to believe a person of his intelligence could behave so stupidly. My first impulse was to track him down and put him out of his misery. I have been afraid that something like this would happen but I didn't know how to hold it off. I talk to him and caution him about potential problems but he never seems to be able to find out in any way but the hard way. I was not aware of the fact that he had a drinking problem. I still won't know the facts until I talk to him. That will be awhile because he is doing an antique show in Kalamazoo, Michigan.

According to the paper, Scott is very fortunate to have had both the fine and the jail sentence suspended. He will be on probation for a year with restricted driving privileges. I am thankful that he did not have an accident that injured him or someone else. God, I am becoming a regular Pollyanna. There I am finding the bright side when I should take a broom handle to his backside. What a great way for the son of an English teacher to behave. They always say that preachers' and teachers' kids are the worst. Scott may make a believer out of me.

I could say that when it rains it pours but that is much too trite. It does seem like the circle of madness continues. At least I am taking it in my stride. He is twenty-one so at most I will only be able to talk to him. Somehow I wish you could talk to him but that is wistful thinking. Drinking and

217

driving seem like father-and-son talk but I will try. I have the feeling that Scott and I will be screaming at each other the next time he comes over. At least he will know that one of us cares. I am not sure that I will be able to face what this will do to the cost of the car insurance but I will try. This was not the way to start my day. I only hope that yours was equally disturbing.

Love,
Adrianne

January 19, 1975

Dear Andrew,

Writing is bcoming more and more interesting. If I ever get a manuscript finished, I am going to take a chance and mail it to a publisher. Wouldn't it be ironic if I could write a best seller and become moderately wealthy? Truth is always stranger than fiction so I suppose that it could happen.

If I ever make any money from writing there are two things I plan to do first. I will buy Leslie a horse of her very own. She has always wanted one, and I would like to see that she has one. Second, I would like to take Doris on a trip to Italy. Doris has been a widow for about five years longer than I have been divorced. She has been a very good friend who has had her share of problems. I think it would do us both a world of good to pick up our passports and head for Italy.

If one Italian could turn me on with a smile and a kiss, certainly a countryful of them would boggle my mind. I told Doris that we would pick up a couple of gigolos and see if they could jiggle. I am not sure what kind of an agency would supply us with willing escorts but I imagine if I had the money it could be arranged. We could pick out a couple for each of us and hold back a couple more for reserve. Then we could get patted on the patio and pinched on the piazza. From there we would improvise and see what would happen.

I would like to walk into an Italian agency and say: "Line up the mature men!" Then Doris and I would walk down the line and say: "I'll take that one for my breakfast date, the little cute one for luncheon, the tall one for dinner, and the big burly one for dessert." What a wonderful way to go! Italians are so charming that I don't even think I would care if they spoke English. We could use gestures and sign language as long as they kept smiling and kissing. I dream of being wealthy enough to have my own male harem. I wonder if that would make me a female chauvinist pig? If I had that kind of money I wouldn't care what they called me.

At least I don't spend all of my time dreaming about the way it was. Now I am dreaming about the way it may be. There must be something exciting around the next corner, and I am more than ready to find it. Someday, Andrew, you may discover that you miss me. When you do, you will find it is too late. I am becoming the liberated woman, and I like it.

Freely,
Adrianne

P.S. I know I'm free. I had dinner at a restaurant and I left a tip for the waitress.

February 5, 1975

Dear Andrew,

Three years ago we were divorced, and I wrote my first letter. Tonight I am writing my last letter. I no longer need to type letters as an emotional release. I've been to hell and back. I still don't have all the answers, but now I know that what is more, I don't even have all the questions. I've learned to live without you or in spite of you. Love doesn't end but marriage does. Divorce is a type of death. The man I love is gone and what lives in his name has no meaning for me. My Andrew will always be young, compassionate, and loving. The good he gave will grow in the children we created. I will remember the things in the past that I will choose: those will be the good times. This is what three years have done for me. They have given me objectivity. Oh, the pain is there but it is wrapped in layers and put in its proper place. I thought I'd be free if I could hate you. This was wrong. Hate only hurts everyone involved. Life is too precious to waste on hate.

Now I know that I am a whole person. The living hell you put me through was because of your inadequacies as a person and as a man. Because I was a woman, a wife, and a mother, I accepted everything as my fault, my shortcomings, and my inadequacies. I tortured and blamed myself in countless sleepless nights and zombie-like days. I carried the hurt, the guilt, and the fear of having been less than a wife, mother, and woman. Today, I know that I have faults and fears but I also know that they are acceptable. I am a normal, average, complete person with hang-ups, frustrations, and desires. I'm a mixture and this is OK. I'm sorry that it took me three years to come back to life.

For you, the man that exists as Andrew, I have only sympathy. Something became twisted in a good man, and I can't believe that your life can be anything but warped and ugly. I hope you find some satisfaction in your life because you paid the ultimate price. You gave up my love that was honest and true. You gave up your immortality as a father and as a future grandfather. You missed seeing our children move from childhood into adulthood. You lost the respect of your professional peers. I can't believe that your bi-sexual world, complete with understanding waitress, will ever compensate for what you gave up. Maybe I'm wrong and maybe you are happy in the only way you can be happy. I'll never know because our lives can never again meet and merge in any meaningful way.

I only know that today when I saw you across the aisle in a store, you were a stranger with a grim, set jaw and the saddest eyes I've ever seen. I could only smile and walk away.

There's a trite old saying that life begins at forty. I'm forty-one, and I choose to believe it. There's a bright wonderful world out there, and I am going to be a part of it. I'm going to reach out and touch stars. There are airplanes to ride, books to write, smiles to share, children to teach, future grandchildren to spoil, places to go, and best of all—people to meet. Today I can say without regret, "Good-bye, Andrew. Hello, world!"

Sincerely,
Adrianne